Behavioral Health Protocols for Recreational Therapy

Karen Grote, MS, CTRS
Michael Hasl, BA, RTR
Robert Krider, MS, CTRS
Dianne Martin Mortensen, M.Ed., CTRS

Published and distributed by

Idyll Arbor, Inc.

PO Box 720, Ravensdale, WA 98051 (206) 432-3231

Publisher's Note:

We have promoted the development and publishing of this book because we feel that those who use the services of a recreational therapist deserve the best possible care. This book was written for recreational therapy professionals (Certified Therapeutic Recreation Specialists) and for licensed recreational therapists.

To the best of our knowledge, the information and recommendations of this book reflect currently accepted practice. Nevertheless, they can not be considered absolute and universal. Recommendations for therapy for a particular individual must be considered in light of the individual's needs and condition. The authors and publisher disclaim responsibility for any adverse effects resulting directly or indirectly from the suggested protocols, from any undetected errors or from the reader's misunderstanding of the text.

The final chapter of this book includes sample individualized goals, objective and interventions that can be used in designing problem-centered interdisciplinary treatment plans for patients. Portions of this chapter were originally published independently as **Sample Therapeutic Recreation Treatment Plans for Therapeutic Recreation** (1990), by Karen Grote. Although some day behavioral health programs may dispense with individualized treatment plans in favor of interdisciplinary critical pathways, there is currently a continuing need for competence in this area. An addition to the original book is the inclusion of "Terms to Aid Documentation" at the end of each set of treatment plans.

ISBN 1-882883-17-9

For Bernie Thorn

Teacher, Leader, Colleague, Friend

Portions of the royalties from sales of this book go to the Bernie Thorn Efficacy Research Fund of the American Therapeutic Recreation Foundation to support further research.

Contents

Introduction

This book was written to help the recreational therapist create and use critical pathways, protocols and treatment plans as a framework for the services s/he provides. Critical pathways provide the team's overall framework for treatment. Protocols are the building blocks for critical pathways. Taken as a whole, protocols make up the critical pathway. Treatment plans are the individualized treatment goals for each patient. These treatment plans are used to modify protocols to best meet the individual patient's needs. Within this book the therapist will find information on all three elements of patient treatment programs: critical pathways, protocols and treatment plans.

The critical pathway is the overall outline of the treatments and services to be provided by the entire treatment team. The critical pathway starts from a known diagnosis and shows the types of interventions that will be used during treatment.

In many ways a critical pathway is like a highway map. It shows generally how to get from one state to another state. Unlike city maps which show every street and maybe the location of each park, school or public building of interest, the critical pathway "map" provides the reader with just the general route required to get were one wants to go.

A protocol describes the details of the interventions in the critical pathway. Therapists and patients work together to choose the best protocols (e.g. relaxation techniques, cooking skills, social etiquette) to satisfy each part of the critical pathway.

A protocol may be compared to the city map. It outlines which city streets the patient will be taking and maybe even which gas stations or bus stops will be used on the way from "Point A" to "Point B".

A treatment care plan contains the specific instructions for each patient which is meant to help achieve the desired outcome. Using the analogy of the city map and gas station or bus stops, imagine a van full of six patients. When the van stops at the gas station, one patient may need to use the rest room, one may need to buy something to quench her thirst, a third patient may need to use that time to call back to the unit to check in, while the other three have no specific requirements for their time at the gas station.

The protocol may be related to the use of the community center. The treatment plans within the protocol could be as follows. One patient may need to improve his ability to empty his bladder on a regular schedule. Another patient may need to remember to drink fluids on a regular basis to avoid dehydration that causes complications with prescribed medications. The third patient may need to check in as part of learning not to wander away from the group. The other three patients may have treatment plans which require other specific performance on other parts of the outing. The protocol would be the purpose of the community center outing and the treatment care plan would be the specific requirements for each patient while they are enrolled in the protocol.

This type of planning and program documentation may be new to the therapist. During the 1980s, the content of medical documentation in behavioral health care settings remained relatively unchanged. Influenced heavily by the Joint Commission on Accreditation of Health Organizations, the chart of a mental health patient included patient assessment, individualized interdisciplinary treatment plans and annotated narrative progress notes.

By the middle of the last decade, new ways of thinking about treatment began to invade our health care system. New ideas like protocols, standardized treatment plans, standards of care and critical pathways were used. These are now a standard part of accepted clinical practice. They are designed to standardize and define appropriate treatment and to in some way predict what outcome is expected.

Health care facilities are turning to the use of critical pathways and treatment protocols to help streamline the services they provide. Using them tends to improve the quality of services and reduces the overall cost of the delivery of those services.

The therapist finds himself/herself needing to select or develop protocols which fit into the facility's critical pathways. Once this is done, s/he can then write a patient treatment plan which complements both the critical pathway and protocol.

The three sections of this book discuss critical pathways, protocols and treatment plans in more detail. Examples of each are provided which the therapist can use in his/her facility to improve his/her quality of care.

Critical Pathways

The use of critical pathways is a recent addition to health care settings. The *critical path*, as it is often called, describes a prescribed and expected course of hospitalization for patients with similar problems. The earliest use of critical pathways in hospitals occurred sometime in the early 1980s in medical and surgical areas. It was almost a decade before psychiatric departments began to be concerned with the development of critical pathways. Some hospitals refer to them as *clinical pathways* today. A pathway includes a day-by-day schedule of treatment events, usually designed as a chart. Protocols that are discipline-specific may be used to contribute to this interdisciplinary document.

In the rapidly changing and reform-conscious health care market, the use of critical pathways is driven by two concurrent forces. On the one hand, managed care insurance companies want to be able to predict the length and course of hospitalization for specific diagnoses. They use critical paths to evaluate the hospital's cost efficiency in the delivery of accepted and appropriate quality care.

The other factor that is placing greater emphasis on the use of critical pathways is the hospital's effort to remain competitive in a market which is remarkably unstable. The hospital is forced to streamline treatment to stay competitive. There was a time when hospitals didn't tell physicians how to practice. This is no longer true. The physician is expected to implement treatments and services which address patients' needs in the most effective manner. These treatments and services are to be based on scientific studies which support their benefit and are to comply with professional standards of practice. The once-sacred right of the physician to keep a patient hospitalized as long as s/he wanted and to order as many tests as desired is no longer acceptable.

Protocols and critical pathways predict expected outcomes during a standardized course of treatment. Doctors whose practice of medicine falls outside these standards are asked to conform to reasonable and accepted norms or risk sanctions.

The same standards are being applied to all health care providers. The goal is to give quality care to patients while increasing cost efficiency by avoiding unnecessary care.

Since critical paths are interdisciplinary, they describe each discipline's contribution to the course of events of a patient's hospitalization. Where they are in use in common practice, they serve as a framework for communication and daily assignments. They are used at treatment team rounds or shift reports to evaluate the patient's progress along the path. When discrepancies exist between the path and the actual implementation of it, problem solving is initiated to resolve the deviations and resume the patient's recovery. Students, interns, volunteers and new employees can also use critical pathways as educational tools to learn the facility's methods, practice habits and anticipated outcomes.

A critical pathway charts a prescribed and expected course of hospitalization or treatment for patients with the same diagnoses and treatment plans. Thus, there will be one critical pathway written for patients with major affective disorder, another for those who have schizophrenic disorders and another for patients with bipolar disorders.

The pathway identifies the diagnosis, the anticipated length of stay and the expected outcomes for the patient when the path is followed. A day-by-day list of required tasks is recorded in a number of categories. These will typically include assessments, tests, medication, intervention strategies, teaching needs and discharge planning. The contributions of each discipline are needed for a comprehensive pathway.

The physician will order standard testing for each diagnosis, as well as other tests that are deemed necessary for the individual patient. The time requirements for completing assessments by each discipline will be noted on the pathway. Nursing has standard requirements for assessing vital signs and the behavioral status of patients that are written into the plan. Treatment interventions, including group or individual counseling, will be there. Many patients also need additional education and discharge planning and this will be included as well.

Vital to the development of the pathway is the determination of anticipated outcomes for the patient. Without the outcome, there is no way to determine the efficacy of treatment that is achieved by following the plan. Today hospitals and third party payers are critically concerned with three outcomes: providing quality care, maintaining cost effectiveness and avoiding unnecessary treatment. Procedures or outcomes that fall outside the prescribed pathway may be seen as too expensive or unnecessary for the care of the patient.

Every discipline should be represented — medicine, nursing, social service, recreational therapy, occupational therapy, as well as educational services for adolescents, psychology when used regularly for testing or treatment and perhaps dietary when needed.

This book includes only one example of a critical pathway. Aside from minor changes due to severity of illness, there usually is little variation in the recreational therapy contributions to critical pathways. For example, the recreational therapy department may require an assessment within the first day of hospitalization for someone who is depressed, but may not be expected to complete the assessment until the second or third day for those who are hospitalized with schizophrenic disorders because they may not be able to participate in an evaluation immediately.

Another variation may include not requiring a leisure discharge plan for patients who are admitted with Alzheimer's disease or related dementias. On the other hand, the pathway for someone with Alzheimer's disease may include teaching the family appropriate activities for patients who will return home.

Critical pathways are a visual image of standards of care and departmental policies and procedures that pertain to direct patient care. While nurses and doctors may be the most familiar with the use of critical pathways, it is also important that the recreational therapist and all other practitioners become acquainted with their use and design. A example of a critical pathway for depression is shown on the following two pages.

Critical Pathway: Depression

Estimated Length of Stay: 7 Days

Procedure	Day 1	Day 2	Day 3	Day 4

Assessment and Monitoring	MD assessment in 24 hours
	History & physical by resident
	SCL-90-R symptom checklist
	Nursing assessment:
	  Vital signs PRN
	  Potential for suicide
	  Dietary needs
		Mental status exam PRN
		SS to complete family assessment
		Family meeting PRN
		Complete RT and OT assessment
		→ → →
		→ → →
		Monitor self-care
		Monitor diet/fluid balance PRN
		Monitor activity level
			→ → →
			→ → →
			→ → →
			→ → →
			
			→ → →
				→ → →
				→ → →
				→ → →
				→ → →
				
				→ → →

Planning		Treatment team meeting Individualized treatment plan Initiate discharge plan		
Consults	Medical PRN Dietary PRN Child Psychiatrist PRN			
Tests	CBC Chem20 Profile Urinalysis Urine pregnancy test PRN Urine toxic screen PRN Optional: T4, TSH, RPR, CXR, EKG	MMPI PRN Optional: MRI, EEG, dexamethasone suppression		
Treatments	Milieu as tolerated Open groups as tolerated Individual psychotherapy 1:1 Supportive care	Milieu therapy Assigned groups → → → → → →	→ → → → → → → → → → → →	→ → → → → → → → → → → →
Medication	Orders PRN Monitor medication for compliance and side effects	→ → → → → →	→ → → → → →	→ → → → → →
Teaching	Orientation to unit Orientation to program			

Admission Date: _____

Procedure	Day 5	Day 6	Day 7	Patient Outcomes
Assessment and Monitoring	→ → → → → → → → → → → → → → →	→ → → → → → → → → → → → → → →	Retaking of SCL-90-R → → → → → → → → → → → → → → →	Patient will have comprehensive evaluation and effective monitoring of progress.
Planning	Leisure discharge planning		Completion of discharge plan	Patient will participate in discharge planning and be satisfied with plan.
Consults		BVR referral PRN		Patient will have referrals as needed for follow up.
Tests				Patient will have adequate evaluation of medical status.
Treatments	→ → → → → → → → → → → →	→ → → → → → → → → → → →	→ → → → → → → → → → → →	Patient will have remission of severe depressive symptoms.
Medication	→ → → → → →	→ → → → → →	→ → → → → →	Patient will accept and comply with medication as prescribed.
Teaching		Self-medication PRN	Review discharge plans Medication teaching	Patient will state increased understanding of depression, treatment and outcomes.

Abbreviations and References for the Critical Pathway — Depression

BVR (Bureau of Vocational Rehabilitation) A government agency that assists people in vocational training and locating jobs. The actual name of this agency may be different depending on the state that the therapist is working in and depending on whether the agency is a federal or state agency.

CBC (Complete Blood Count) This test determines the number of red and white blood cells, platelets and other blood elements and compares those numbers to the actual volume of blood. The medical staff can use these numbers to detect infection and other abnormalities. This test helps the team identify other possible secondary diagnoses.

Chem20 Profile This is a blood test which consists of a series of 20 lab tests of blood enzymes. The purpose of the test is to help identify organic causes of mental illness.

CXR (Chest X-Ray) A chest x-ray is ordered to help identify whether the patient has tuberculosis.

Dexamethasone Suppression Test A test which evaluates the function of the hypothalamic-pituitary-adrenocortical glands. Levels of specific plasma cortisol levels can indicate the presence of organically induced depression and may provide clues to the origin of the problem.

EEG (Electroencephalogram) A test which measures the brain's spontaneous bio-electrical activity. Certain patterns are associated with seizure activity, tumors, infections, or other metabolism dysfunctions.[1]

EKG (Electrocardiogram) A non-invasive test which measures the electrical activity of the patient's heart. The results are printed out on a graph. An EKG may be able to identify patients who would be at increased risk of a cardiac damage if they were to participate in a strenuous exercise program.

Mental Status Exam An evaluation of the patient's mental status (reality orientation, confusion, delusions/hallucinations).

Milieu Therapy A term which implies that you are intentionally using the entire environment in your therapy. In a therapeutic setting, the milieu (environment) is structured to meet the emotional, health, social and other needs of the patient.

MMPI (Minnesota Multiphasic Personality Inventory) The MMPI assesses individual personality traits. The test is a 566 item true-false test of ten different areas related to personality: hypochondriasis, depression, hysteria, psychopathic-deviate,

---

[1]burlingame, j. 1995. **Glossary for Therapists**. Ravensdale, WA: Idyll Arbor, Inc.

masculinity-femininity, paranoia, psychasthenia, schizophrenia, hypomania and social introversion. This test is self-administered by the patient and is available in 45 languages allowing the patient to take the test in his/her native language.

MRI (Magnetic Resonance Imaging) A test, similar to a CAT Scan, which produces a clear picture of the internal components of the body. The MRI uses a magnetic field instead of radiation to make three-dimensional images.

Open Groups Activity groups offered on the unit which are available to all patients without requiring a physician's order or other referrals.

OT (Occupational Therapy) The services offered by an individual who has completed all of the training and exams required by the American Occupational Therapy Certification Board (AOTCB) or who has met state requirements to be called an "Occupational Therapist".

Potential for Suicide An assessment of the patient's preoccupation with suicidal thoughts. Specific aspects of the patient's thought process and the degree to which any suicide plan is thought out are evaluated to determine the patient's potential for suicide.

PRN (as needed) A short hand abbreviation used in health care fields which means that a service, therapy or medication may be given to the patient as his/her need dictates.

RPR (Rapid Plasma Reagin Test) A group of tests for syphilis using specific techniques to stain the sample to allow the identification of syphilis without a microscope.

RT (Recreational Therapy) The services offered by an individual who has completed all of the training and exams required by the National Council for Therapeutic Recreation Certification (NCTRC) or who has met state requirements to be called a "Recreational Therapist".

SCL-90-R (Symptom Checklist-90-Revised) This test evaluates the symptoms of psychological distress felt by the patient. This 90 item paper-pencil, self-administered assessment is often used for psychological screening, evaluation and treatment planning in mental health settings. The SCL-90-R divides symptoms into nine dimensions: somatization, obsessive-compulsive, interpersonal sensitivity, depression, anxiety, hostility, phobic anxiety, paranoid ideation, and psychoticism. The test also provides the staff with three global indicators of distress: global severity index, positive symptom index and positive symptom total.

Self Care The ability of a patient to care for personal hygiene, grooming and other tasks of daily living.

Self Medication The ability of a patient to correctly administer his/her own medications.

T4 Measurement of the T4 levels of serum thyroid hormone in the body. The clinical manifestations of low serum levels are similar to clinical depression: fatigue, forgetfulness, decreasing mental stability and slowed reflex relaxation time (motor retardation).

TSH (Thyroid-Stimulating Hormone) Measurement of the levels of TSH produced by the pituitary gland. The clinical manifestations of inadequate levels of TSH are similar to clinical depression: fatigue, forgetfulness, decreasing mental stability and slowed reflex relaxation time (motor retardation).

Urinalysis This test is used two ways: it may be used to identify possible infections or biological malfunctions or it may be used to identify traces of substances such as alcohol, barbiturates, cocaine, etc.

Urine Toxic Screen A urine toxic screen may be done to identify traces of substances such as alcohol and other drugs ingested within a specific time period. This time period varies depending on the substance, as each substance has a different average time to clear out of the urine. Alcohol may clear out of the urine in 7 - 12 hours, where barbiturates will take 24 hours for short-acting barbiturates and up to 3 weeks for long-acting barbiturates.

Vital Signs The four basic measurable functions of health are called vital signs: 1. blood pressure, 2. pulse, 3. respiration, and 4. temperature.[2]

---

[2]burlingame, j. 1995. **Glossary for Therapists**. Ravensdale, WA: Idyll Arbor, Inc.

Protocols

The critical pathway is the facility's master plan for each type of patient. Each critical pathway is made up of protocols — the building blocks which fit into the structure of the critical pathway. A protocol is a written plan which outlines:

1. who is to take part in a treatment
2. what specific treatment will be offered and
3. what changes the patient should see as a result of the treatment.

This chapter will help the therapist become acquainted with two different kinds of protocols — diagnostic protocols and program protocols.

There are many things that contribute to the need for protocol development in recreational therapy. Some of the most pressing reasons to use protocols are for cost-effective treatment, the need to moderate the effect of geographic variation in academic training and clinical practice, and the need to further establish a research-supported body of common practice.

In the recreational therapy literature, several authors have discussed protocol development. Knight and Johnson (1989) wrote that "protocols are a group of strategies or actions initiated in response to a problem, an issue or a symptom of a patient." Olsson (1990) defined a protocol as "a set of very specific instructions, regulations and requirements that govern an agency's recreational therapy practice and when implemented produce specific treatment outcomes." Ferguson (1991) further added "protocols provide information detailing the specific problem or need to be addressed and provide a set of expected outcomes which can be measured and examined."

There are four kinds of protocols: diagnostic, symptom specific, activity and program. Each type of protocol has its own purpose, strengths and weaknesses. The health care professional can use the type of protocol or combinations of protocols which best addresses the patent's need and the facility's needs.

A diagnostic protocol describes what treatment is offered to patients who have the specific diagnosis. For instance, they describe what modalities you use with a person who has a schizophrenic disorder. The idea behind diagnostic protocols is that most patients with a similar diagnosis should have similar needs. The recreational therapist draws upon the strength of the protocols to address the primary needs of the patient diagnostic group. For the recreational therapist with a mix of patient diagnoses these protocols may not be ideal because the psychosocial deficiencies and needs demonstrated by one patient may be significantly different from other patients on the same unit. These protocols may also be called teaching protocols. You will find examples of diagnostic protocols in the next section of this book.

At times the therapist will find it better to design treatment protocols around the actual symptoms exhibited by the patient. That way patients with different diagnoses but similar needs (e.g., anger management) may be placed in group therapy sessions together. This type of protocol, symptom protocol, is written to describe appropriate treatment offered in response to very specific symptomatology displayed by the patient. These may also be referred to as functionally based protocols. The last section of this book contains treatment plans based on symptomatology. The sample recreational therapy treatment plans in this book may be used to develop symptom protocols. Once the therapist has added the necessary structure to the symptomatology based treatment plans to create protocols, s/he may submit them for agency approval and standardization within the facility.

A third type of protocol is the activity protocol. An activity protocol is the written description of an individual (isolated) activity. This description outlines the scope of the activity, how it is to be taught or run, how the patient's demonstrated skill is to be evaluated and the patient's expected outcome at the end of the activity. An example of an activity protocol would be to teach the patient how to work his/her way through a voice mail system. (Many patients have a hard time when faced with having to make choices from those presented by the phone answering systems. They get confused as they are cascaded through the various choices on the way to being able to leave voice mail.)

Activity protocols can be written to provide structured procedures for each activity that is included within a program protocol. The recreational therapist will find may activities already written up which need only slight modification to become activity protocols. These "canned" activities include relaxation techniques, videos exercise tapes, recipes in cookbooks and many other activities which the therapist may want to use as part of his/her treatment/service. The **Community Integration Program** (Armstrong and Lauzen, 1994) is one of the better known sets of activity protocols in the field of recreational therapy.

A program protocol describes each program that you offer. Your programs may include just one or two related activities (stretching and cardiovascular activity) or they may include unlimited activity choices (paper crafts to enhance expression). The unifying element is that all the activities selected will help the patient toward the desired outcome. Program protocols should include structure (what treatment is provided), process (what the therapist will do in the process) and outcome criteria (what outcomes the patient can expect from the treatment).

Types of Protocols in Health Care

Type of Protocol	Example of Protocol
diagnostic	depression
symptom	uncontrolled anger outbursts
activity	cooking pizza
program	aquatics

Smith-Marker (1988) looked at protocols in a different way in the nursing literature and identified three types: independent, collaborative and interdependent protocols. Independent protocols were discipline-specific, collaborative were written by two disciplines that would co-treat or team-treat patients with common modalities and the interdependent protocols were interdisciplinary and required a physician's order to initiate treatment for a given patient.

Physicians design agency-specific diagnostic protocols. These protocols identify the known etiology and symptomatology as outlined in the current **Diagnostic and Statistical Manual of Mental Disorders (DSM)**, the accepted treatment practices among that group of physicians and the expected outcomes when following the protocol.

This current book offers two kinds of protocols: diagnostic and program protocols. All the examples in this book are written as independent or discipline-specific protocols for recreational therapists. Whenever collaborative or interdependent protocols are needed at a particular agency, the examples here can serve as a starting point or guide to successful team efforts.

Although it is not yet in the standards of practice for recreational therapists, each recreational therapy department should begin to draft standardized program protocols. Most departments already have some form of group descriptions; they may be updated to resemble the kinds of examples in this book. Program protocols should include structure, process and outcome criteria. They should also consider referral considerations, contraindications, risk management issues and any specific personnel training or certification requirement (e.g., a Water Safety Instructor certification). The department may choose to start this process by using nationally standardized treatment protocols like the **Community Integration Program (CIP)** or the **Leisure Step Up** and then add the structure and necessary processes to their own departmental policies and procedures.

Departments also need to design diagnostic protocols for frequently treated diagnostic groups. This step is important for establishing a common practice among therapists who work in a department, so that patients know what treatment outcomes they can expect in the program regardless of which therapist is assigned to treat them. Other professionals can also come to depend on the standardized delivery of services.

Protocols, no matter what kind, should be well thought out and based on both the therapist's clinical experience and on the experience and research of others. Whenever possible, diagnostic and program protocols for recreational therapy should be annotated with outcome findings from efficacy research. It is critical in our field that we continue to support and conduct research to identify appropriate interventions which achieve expected outcomes.

Diagnostic Protocols

A diagnostic protocol is an outline of the treatment and services routinely provided to patients with a specific diagnosis. The protocol is defined by an outline with five parts:
1. diagnostic category,
2. assessment criteria,
3. symptoms typically observed,
4. protocol criteria and
5. a bibliography of supporting literature.

In behavioral medicine settings most of the diagnostic protocols will be from the diagnoses found in the most current edition of **Diagnostic and Statistical Manual of Mental Disorders (DSM)**. The diagnosis makes up the first part of the diagnostic protocol outline.

The second part of the diagnostic protocol outline contains the types of assessments the therapist completes prior to "admitting" a patient to that particular protocol. The therapist should select the appropriate internal and standardized forms for assessing the patient's status through the use of his/her clinical judgment, through guidance found in the diagnostic protocol itself and through compliance with facility and professional standards. The assessment helps establish a baseline which can be used to measure changes in the patient as treatment progresses.

It is important that the therapist make some kind of determination about the patient's status before admitting him/her to a diagnostic protocol. There will always be patients who have been given a specific diagnosis but who are inappropriate for inclusion in the protocol. An example might be a patient with the diagnosis of major depressive episode who also has a second diagnosis of autism. That patient would not be able to benefit from most of the interventions outlined in the protocol.

Another type of criteria listed in the second part of the outline is related to ongoing or specific evaluations which take place during the course of a diagnostic protocol. The purpose of a post-admission evaluation is to measure how far the patient has moved from his/her baseline and/or to determine discharge.

The third part of the diagnostic protocol outline is the symptom list. In behavioral medicine the symptom list is easy to complete since the **DSM** lists pertinent symptoms for each diagnosis. The therapist will want to list symptoms from the **DSM** which relate to the patient's ability to have a functional leisure lifestyle and which are responsive to recreational therapy intervention. The therapist will also want to add symptoms which are common within the diagnostic group and which impact the patient's ability to perform other advanced activities of daily living.

The fourth part of the diagnostic protocol outline has two parts: *process* criteria and *outcome* criteria. Process refers to the steps taken and services provided by the therapist to complete the protocol. This part leads the therapist through the treatment from its inception to its completion. The process part of the diagnostic protocol outline should be written in such a way that consistency between therapists is provided.

The outcome criteria are the measurable changes brought about in the patient as a direct result of being admitted to the protocol. With each treatment or service (process) there should be a change (outcome) which is the direct result of the specific treatment or service.

The last part of the diagnostic protocol outline is the listing of specific books, articles, and other professional material which supports the efficacy of the treatment or service being provided. References which help identify specific needs and characteristics of patients within the diagnostic group should also be listed.

The following page shows a sample format for diagnostic protocols. The pages after the format contain four examples of diagnostic protocols. The therapist is encouraged to use these as a framework for developing a facility-specific set of diagnostic protocols. These protocols will probably need to be modified to fit your facility's system of treatment delivery. You will also find that your diagnostic protocols may need to be updated periodically to keep up with patient variations and new scientific data.

Sample Diagnostic Protocol Form

I. Diagnosis State the specific diagnostic group from the current edition of the **Diagnostic and Statistical Manual for Mental Disorders**.
II. Assessment Criteria Identify how the patient with this diagnosis will be assessed, what information will be gathered and what standardized assessment should be used.
III. Symptoms List the cluster of psychiatric symptoms that are used to accurately diagnose a patient with this disorder. Add any additional common psychosocial symptoms that may be addressed through recreational therapy.

IV. Process Criteria	**IV. Outcome Criteria**
Identify the steps the therapist will take to assess and treat this type of patient. Consider all relevant and appropriate modalities that will be used in the treatment plan.	State the outcomes the patient can expect after s/he is treated by a recreational therapist who employs this protocol.

V. Bibliography Record the bibliographical references used to develop this protocol.

Major Depressive Episode
Diagnostic Protocol

I. Diagnosis

Major Depressive Episode

II. Assessment Criteria

The assessment includes an evaluation of the patient's cognitive, social and physical functioning, including the patient's motivation, leisure interests and patterns of participation. The agency's screening assessment may be followed by administering the *Leisure Motivation Scale*, the *Leisure Diagnostic Battery*, the *Leisure Interest Measurement*, the *Free Time Boredom Measure* and/or the *Leisurescope Plus*, as indicated.

III. Symptoms

A patient diagnosed with major depression will experience five or more of the following symptoms:
- depressed mood
- diminished interest or pleasure
- significant weight loss or gain
- insomnia or hypersomnia
- psychomotor agitation or retardation
- fatigue or loss of energy
- feelings of worthlessness or inappropriate guilt
- difficulty concentrating or making decisions
- recurrent thoughts of death

In addition, such a patient may also exhibit:
- a lack of initiative for usual activities
- diminished social interaction
- inadequate assertive social skills

IV. Process Criteria	IV. Outcome Criteria
The recreational therapist develops an individualized treatment plan, considering all subjective and objective assessment information and provides treatment to the patient from among the following modalities:	At the completion of treatment the patient will be able to:
1. exercise	1. report increased level of energy
2. stress management and relaxation therapy	2a. demonstrate increased self-regulation ability 2b. identify a plan to use effective stress reduction techniques to reduce level of stress
3. leisure education	3a. report awareness of benefits of leisure participation 3b. identify a personal leisure plan for use after discharge
4. friendship development	4a. identify strategies for increasing social supports 4b. demonstrate increased social initiative
5. structured tasks	5. demonstrate improved concentration and decision-making
6. assertiveness training	6. demonstrate appropriate assertive communication skills

V. Bibliography

American Psychiatric Association. 1994. **Diagnostic and Statistical Manual of Mental Disorders (Fourth Edition)**. Washington, D.C.

Compton, D. M. and S. E. Iso-Ahola (Eds.) 1994. **Leisure and Mental Health**. Park City, UT: Family Development Resources, Inc.

Coyle, C. P., W. B. Kinney, B. Riley and J. W. Shank. 1991. **Benefits of Therapeutic Recreation: A Consensus View**. Ravensdale, WA: Idyll Arbor, Inc.

Dehn, D. 1995. **Leisure Step Up**. Ravensdale, WA: Idyll Arbor, Inc.

Eisler, R. M., M. Hersen and P. M. Miller. 1974. "Shaping components of Assertive Behavior with Instruction and Feedback." *American Journal of Psychiatry*. 131, 1344-1347.

Epperson, A., P. A. Witt and G. Hitzhusen. 1977. **Leisure Counseling: An Aspect of Leisure Education**. Springfield: Charles C. Thomas.

Grossman, A. H. 1976. "Power of Activity in a Treatment Setting." *Therapeutic Recreation Journal*. 10 (4), 119-124.

McGlynn, G. 1987. **Dynamics of Fitness: A Practical Approach**. Dubuque, IA: Wm. C. Brown.

Morgan, W. P. and S. E. Goldston. 1987. **Exercise and Mental Health**. Washington, DC: Hemisphere Publishing.

Schizophrenia and Other Psychotic Disorders
Diagnostic Protocol

I. Diagnosis

Schizophrenia and Other Psychotic Disorders

II. Assessment Criteria

The assessment includes an evaluation of the patient's cognitive, social and physical functioning and also the patient's motivation, leisure skills, interests and patterns of participation. The agency's screening assessment may be followed by the use of *Comprehensive Evaluation in Recreational Therapy (CERT — Psych)*, *Leisure Motivation Scale*, *Leisure Interest Measurement*, *Leisure Attitude Measurement*, *Leisure Diagnostic Battery*, *STILAP* and *Leisurescope Plus*, as indicated.

III. Symptoms

Symptoms typically include:
- delusions
- hallucinations
- disorganized thoughts
- grossly disorganized or catatonic behavior

Also, "negative" symptoms include:
- affect flattening
- diminished capacity for logical thinking
- lack of motivation

Patients with these disorders may also experience:
- social and occupational dysfunction
- concurrent mood disorders
- substance abuse.

IV. Process Criteria	IV. Outcome Criteria
The recreational therapist will develop an individualized treatment plan, considering all subjective and objective information and provide treatment to the patient from among the following modalities:	At the completion of treatment the patient will be able to:
1. exercise	1a. sustain focus with active participation 1b. report increased level of energy
2. stress management	2a. identify and practice techniques to decrease symptoms 2b. identify a plan to use effective means to reduce stress or symptoms after discharge
3. leisure education	3a. report awareness of benefits of leisure participation 3b. identify a personal leisure plan for use after discharge
4. friendship development	4a. identify strategies for increasing social supports 4b. demonstrate increased social initiative
5. structured tasks	5a. demonstrate improved concentration 5b. demonstrate improved decision-making 5c. demonstrate improved follow-through
6. assertiveness training	6. demonstrate appropriate assertive communication skills

V. Bibliography

American Psychiatric Association. 1994. **Diagnostic and Statistical Manual of Mental Disorders (Fourth Edition)**. Washington, DC.

Ascher-Svanum, H. and A. A. Krause. 1991. **Psychoeducational Groups for Patients with Schizophrenia: A Guide for Practitioners**. Rockville: Aspen Publications.

Compton, D. M. and S. E. Iso-Ahola (Eds.) 1994. **Leisure and Mental Health**. Park City, UT: Family Development Resources, Inc.

Coyle, C. P., W. B. Kinney, B. Riley and J. W. Shank. 1991. **Benefits of Therapeutic Recreation: A Consensus View**. Ravensdale, WA: Idyll Arbor, Inc.

Dehn, D., 1995. **Leisure Step Up**. Ravensdale, WA: Idyll Arbor, Inc.

Eisler, R. M., M. Hersen and P. M. Miller. 1974. "Shaping components of Assertive Behavior with Instruction and Feedback." *American Journal of Psychiatry*. 131, 1344-1347.

Epperson, A., P. A. Witt and G. Hitzhusen. 1977. **Leisure Counseling: An Aspect of Leisure Education**. Springfield: Charles C. Thomas.

Grossman, A. H. 1976. "Power of Activity in a Treatment Setting." *Therapeutic Recreation Journal*. 10 (4), 119-124.

McGlynn, G. 1987. **Dynamics of Fitness: A Practical Approach**. Dubuque, IA: Wm. C. Brown.

Morgan, W. P. and S. E. Goldston. 1987. **Exercise and Mental Health**. Washington, DC: Hemisphere Publishing.

Dementia of the Alzheimer's Type
Diagnostic Protocol

I. Diagnosis

Dementia of the Alzheimer's Type

II. Assessment Criteria

Cognitive functioning is evaluated related to memory impairment. Patient's social and physical functioning are also evaluated including evaluation of significant past leisure interests. The agency's screening assessment may be followed by the use of the *Mini Mental State Test*, the *Therapeutic Recreation Activity Assessment (TRAA)* or the *Ohio Functional Assessment Battery*, as indicated.

III. Symptoms

Dementia of the Alzheimer's type is marked by the following symptoms:

1. the development of multiple cognitive deficits manifested by both memory impairment and one of the following: aphasia, apraxia or agnosia
2. disturbance in executive functioning, e.g., planning, organizing, sequencing, abstracting
3. social and occupational functional impairment represented by a decline from a previous level of functioning
4. gradual onset of symptoms
5. continuing cognitive decline

IV. Process Criteria	IV. Outcome Criteria
Dementia of the Alzheimer's type causes progressive decline over the long term. However, in the short term it is possible to see positive changes in patients caused by therapeutic interventions. With that in mind, the recreational therapist will develop an individualized treatment plan, considering all subjective and objective information and provide treatment to the patient from among the following modalities:	At the completion of treatment the patient will be able to:
1. exercise	1a. reduce agitation and control energy level 1b. reduce risk of loss of range of motion
2. reminiscence	2. increase ability to relate to past experiences and verbalize about these experiences
3. validation	3a. decrease negative behavior 3b. improve effective speech
4. sensory stimulation	4. increase ability to respond to stimuli
5. structured tasks	5. increase focus to task
6. socialization activities	6. increase interaction with peers through relevant speech and movement

V. Bibliography

American Psychiatric Association. 1994. **Diagnostic and Statistical Manual of Mental Disorders (Fourth Edition)**. Washington, DC.

Best-Martini, E., M. A. Weeks and P. Wirth. 1994. **Long Term Care: Interpretation and Inspiration for Activity and Social Service Professionals**. Ravensdale, WA: Idyll Arbor, Inc.

Birren, J. E. and Deutchman, D. E. 1991. **Guiding Autobiography Groups for Older Adults**. Baltimore: Johns Hopkins Press.

Daems J. (Ed.) 1994. **Reviews of Research in Sensory Integration**. Torrance: Sensory Integration International.

Feil, N. 1993. **The Validation Breakthrough: Simple Techniques for Communicating with People with Alzheimer's-Type Dementia**. Baltimore: Health Professions Press.

Gallo, J. J., W. Reichel and L. Andersen. 1988. **Handbook of Geriatric Assessment**. Rockville, MD: Aspen Publications.

Hurley, O. 1988. **Safe Therapeutic Exercise for the Frail Elderly: An Introduction**. Albany, NY: The Center for the Study of Aging.

Kane, R. and R. Kane. 1981. **Assessing the Elderly, A Practical Guide to Measurement**. Lexington: Lexington Books.

Kemp, B. 1990. **Geriatric Rehabilitation**. Boston: College-Hill Press.

Keogh-Hoss, M. A. 1994. **Therapeutic Recreation Activity Assessment**. Ravensdale, WA: Idyll Arbor, Inc.

Parker, S. D. and C. Will. 1993. **Activities for the Elderly Volume 2: A Guide to Working with Residents with Significant Physical and Cognitive Disabilities**. Ravensdale, WA: Idyll Arbor, Inc.

Scogin, F. and M. Prohaska. 1993. **Aiding Older Adults with Memory Complaints**. Sarasota: Professional Resource Press.

Zgola, J. M. 1987. **Doing Things: A Guide to Programming Activities for Persons with Alzheimer's Disease and Related Disorders**. Baltimore: Johns Hopkins Press.

Attention Deficit/Hyperactivity Disorder
Diagnostic Protocol

I. Diagnosis

Attention Deficit/Hyperactivity Disorder

II. Assessment Criteria

The assessment includes an evaluation of the patient's cognitive, social and physical functioning, as well as the patient's motivation, leisure interest and patterns of participation. The agency's screening assessment may be followed by the *Leisurescope Plus* (or *Teen Leisurescope Plus*), the *Leisure Motivation Scale*, the *Ohio Functional Assessment Battery, Leisure Interest Survey (CompuTR),* the *Therapeutic Recreation Activity Assessment, Comprehensive Evaluation in Recreational Therapy (CERT — Psych)* or the *School Social Behavioral Scale*, as indicated.

III. Symptoms

A patient diagnosed with Attention Deficit/Hyperactivity Disorder, Combined Type, will experience six or more of the following symptoms of inattention:

- makes careless mistakes
- has difficulty sustaining attention
- does not seem to listen
- does not follow through on instructions
- has difficulty organizing
- does not engage in mental tasks
- loses things
- is easily distracted
- is forgetful

In addition, such a patient will exhibit six or more of the following symptoms of hyperactivity and impulsivity:

- is fidgety
- leaves seat frequently
- runs about excessively
- has difficulty engaging in quiet play
- is often "on the go"
- talks excessively
- blurts out
- has difficulty waiting for a turn
- interrupts/intrudes

This type of patient may also experience:

- low self-esteem
- poor frustration tolerance
- mood lability
- excessive gross motor activity
- inadequate interaction
- non-assertive social skills
- academic problems.

IV. Process Criteria	IV. Outcome Criteria
The recreational therapist will develop an individualized treatment plan, considering all subjective and objective information and provide treatment to the patient from among the following modalities:	At the completion of treatment the patient will be able to:
1. structured tasks	1a. demonstrate improved concentration and decision-making 1b. successfully complete a project
2. social and assertive skills training	2a. demonstrate increased knowledge and skills in self-awareness and social interactions 2b. exhibit improved communication skills and social/cooperative play 2c. demonstrate improved personal hygiene, appearance and social etiquette
3. stress management and relaxation training	3a. demonstrate increased self-regulation ability 3b. identify a plan for effective stress reduction
4. leisure education	4a. report awareness of the benefits of leisure participation 4b. identify a personal leisure plan for use after discharge
5. physical fitness/gross motor activities	5. demonstrate improved level of activity

V. Bibliography

American Psychiatric Association. 1994. **Diagnostic and Statistical Manual for Mental Disorders (Fourth Edition)**. Washington, DC.

Coyle, C. P., W. B., R. Riley and J. Shank (Eds.) 1991. **Benefits of Therapeutic Recreation: A Consensus View**. Ravensdale, WA: Idyll Arbor, Inc.

Davis, M., E. Robbins Eshelman and M. McKay. 1995. **The Relaxation and Stress Reduction Workbook, Fourth Edition**. Oakland, CA: New Harbinger Publications.

Hipp, E. 1985. **Fighting Invisible Tigers: A Stress Management Guide for Teens**. Minneapolis: Free Spirit Publishing.

Hipp, E. 1987. **A Teacher's Guide to Fighting Invisible Tigers: A 12 Part Course in Lifeskills Development**. Minneapolis: Free Spirit Publishing.

Kaufman, G. and L. Raphael. 1990. **Stick Up for Yourself! Every Kid's Guide to Personal Power and Positive Self-Esteem**. Minneapolis: Free Spirit Publishing.

Kaufman, G. and L. Raphael. 1991. **Teacher's Guide to Stick Up for Yourself! A 10 Part Course In Self-Esteem and Assertiveness for Kids**. Minneapolis: Free Spirit Publishing.

Korb, K. L., S. D. Azok and E. A. Leutenberg. 1992. **SEALS + Plus: Self-Esteem and Life Skills: Reproducible Activity-Based Handouts Created for Teachers and Counselors**. Beachwood, OH: Wellness Reproductions, Inc.

Winnick, J. P. (Ed.) 1990. **Adapted Physical Education and Sport**. Champaign: Human Kinetics Books.

Program Protocol

A program protocol is an outline of an activity category such as gardening, aquatics, relaxation techniques or communications skills. The protocol specifies the components of the activity which will be used as the treatment modality.

An example of a component is "stretching and warm-ups". The program protocol does not necessarily say which type of exercise program will be used (e.g., Step, aquatics exercise) but it does list the necessary components which the activity must offer. This allows the therapist to change the exercise program to best meet the needs of the patient. In fact the flexibility allowed in selecting the type of activity is the main difference between a program protocol and an activity protocol. A program protocol allows the therapist flexibility in selecting the activity while an activity protocol specifically states the activity to be used.

The outline in a program protocol has seven parts:
   1. treatment modality
   2. rationale
   3. referral criteria
   4. risk management
   5. protocol criteria
   6. credentialling required by staff
   7. bibliography of supporting material

The first part of the program protocol outline is the identification of a treatment modality category. The term "treatment modality" refers to the type of program used to provide the therapeutic intervention. Using cosmetics (and the instruction on how to apply them) may be an appropriate modality to help increase a patient's hygienic cleanliness. (Cosmetics is the modality.) The instruction on how to use a washing machine is another modality to help increase a patient's hygienic cleanliness. (Washing is the modality.) Both of these would be appropriate activities under the program protocol of "hygiene".

The second part of the program protocol outline is the rationale — a statement about why this intervention is needed. This section also provides documentation (from literature) on why the specific treatment modality is appropriate to use as an intervention. It is vital that this part of the outline is done well. Therapists are finding that they have fewer contact hours with the patient than they did in the past. It is important to ensure that the most expedient and beneficial path of treatment is being provided. The practice of recreational therapy is both an art and a science. To meet health care standards the therapist will need to be able to provide scientifically documented rationales for the interventions being used.

The third part of the program protocol outline is referrals. Not all patients will benefit from participation in the activities of a particular program protocol. This part of the outline provides guidance for both the recreational therapist and the rest of the treatment team as to who is appropriate for this protocol.

The fourth part of the program protocol outline is risk management. This section provides each therapist with a list of identified risks to which the facility or patient may be exposed. Exposure to risk is managed by identifying the risk, structuring the activity to reduce risk and outlining steps to be taken if a risk has been realized.

The fifth part of the program protocol outline has three components: structure criteria, process criteria and outcome criteria.

Structure criteria refers to the mechanics of the activity. It includes:
- how long each part of the activity should take
- how many patients can engage in the activity at one time
- how often the group will meet to participate in this activity
- the staffing ratio.

If specific *activities* are required, these should also be identified (e.g., "walking for the last 10 minutes of the activity" rather than a more generic "ten minutes of cool-down activity".)

Process criteria refers to the actions that the therapist will take. These actions include instruction, discussion, demonstration, observation, assistance, listening, leadership and reinforcement. When the structure criteria outlines a time frame for an activity, the process criteria describes what the therapist will be doing during each segment of the time frame.

Outcome criteria refer to the actions or knowledge that will be demonstrated by the patient. These outcomes are a direct result of the mechanics of the activity (structure) and the actions of the therapist (process).

The sixth part of the program protocol outline is the credentialling criteria for staff implementing the protocol. Often the requirement will be for the staff person to be a certified therapeutic recreation specialist (from the National Council for Therapeutic Recreation Certification) or to hold a valid state license to practice recreational therapy. Because treatment through the use of protocols requires the clinical skills of observation, assessment, *analysis* and *modification*, a therapist is required. (Paraprofessionals may observe and gather data for the assessment process but it requires clinical training at the therapist level to analyze and modify.)

The seventh and last part of the program protocol outline is the bibliography. Because protocols must be based on content found through literature searches, it is important for the therapist to list all of the pertinent material.

The following pages have five samples of program protocols. The therapist is encouraged to use these as a starting point for his/her facility's own set of program protocols. The same outline may be use to develop activity protocols as long as the protocol is written for a specific activity (e.g., **Leisure Step Up** program) and not for a more generic activity category (e.g., leisure education).

Sample Program Protocol Form

I. Treatment Modality
Write in the name of the group or individual program.

II. Rationale
Cite from the current version of the **Diagnostic and Statistical Manual for Mental Disorders** the symptomatology that this program plans to treat. Use citations from available efficacy research to support the need for this program.

III. Referrals
Identify what kinds of patients will participate in this program. Particular diagnostic groups may be cited or patients may be chosen according to assessed needs and symptoms observed. State any contraindications that exist for participation in this group.

IV. Risk Management
Consider what extraordinary organizational risk may be incurred by the health care organization, as well as any unusual personal risks that could be incurred by patients in the program. Suggest ways of controlling the possible risks through careful assessment, observation, procedures or taking immediate action in response to untoward events.

V. Structure Criteria	**V. Process Criteria**	**V. Outcome Criteria**
State the structure for conducting the groups, e.g., length of group, frequency. List the specific treatment modules (if any) to be used in the program.	List what steps the therapist will take, including content of the program and facilitation interventions.	Identify what outcomes the patient may anticipate if they complete the process and content of the group.

VI. Credentialling

Identify what special certifications, clinical privileges or special training the therapist must have to conduct this program.

VII. Bibliography

Record bibliographical references used to develop this protocol.

Fitness Program
Program Protocol

I. Treatment Modality

Fitness Program

II. Rationale

Low energy and fatigue, difficulty concentrating, sleep disorders and psychomotor disturbances are among the symptomatology of affective disorders.

Participation in exercise programs (Greist et al 1979, Taylor et al 1985) has been found to be effective with depressed patients. Sime (1987) found completion of an exercise program resulted in significantly lower depression scores. Martinsen, Medhus and Sandvik (1984) linked significant reductions in depressive thinking, concentration difficulties, sleep disturbances and muscular tension with participation in an aerobic program. A review of the literature (de Vries 1987) indicated substantial agreement that exercise provides a tranquilizing effect.

III. Referrals

Patients will be referred to the fitness program if they exhibit:

1. low energy levels
2. fatigue
3. psychomotor retardation or mild agitation
4. difficulty concentrating
5. sleep disturbances
6. no contraindications based on physical functioning

IV. Risk Management

Patients will be screened for contraindicating conditions, including such things as cardiovascular disease, diabetes, chemical withdrawal, muscular-skeletal injuries and any physiological effects of medication. Medical authorization will be obtained if there are any counterindicated conditions prior to initiating fitness treatment.

Patients will be observed to determine if proper exercise procedures are followed. Any injuries will be reported immediately to the appropriate nursing and/or medical staff and an incident report will be completed.

V. Criteria

Structure Criteria	Process Criteria	Outcome Criteria
The fitness program is conducted for 45 minutes, five days a week, in the recreation center.	The recreational therapist will assure that all patients are medically screened for the intervention and that the space is free of potential hazards.	
Each module includes:	The therapist will:	The patient will:
1. 10 minutes of stretching and warm-up exercises	1a. Teach patients the importance of self-monitoring symptoms. 1b. Instruct patients in the elements of fitness, including the importance of warming-up, benefits of aerobic conditioning, value of consistent practice. 1c. Begin warm ups with exercises for the lower body first to reduce risk of heart attack.	1a. Report no adverse reactions. 1b. Verbalize understanding of the elements of fitness.
2. 25 minutes of low-impact aerobics	2. Lead fitness exercises and observe patients for any adverse reactions.	2a. Experience the benefits of the exercise. 2b. Report no adverse reactions.
3. 10 minutes of walking or light stretching exercises.	3a. Teach patients how to monitor their heart rates in the optimal range. 3b. Discuss opportunities for fitness programs in community. 3c. Observe patients for significant changes in psychosocial functioning.	3a. Be able to take own heart rate and self-monitor. 3b. Identify plans for fitness activities after discharge. 3c. Report decreased symptoms of depression and anxiety.

VI. Credentialling

The therapist will demonstrate relevant training in fitness instruction.

VII. Bibliography

American Psychiatric Association. 1994. **Diagnostic and Statistical Manual of Mental Disorders (Fourth Edition)**. Washington, DC.

Coyle, C. P., W. B. Kinney, R. Riley, J. Shank (Eds.). 1991. **Benefits of Therapeutic Recreation: A Consensus View**. Ravensdale, WA: Idyll Arbor, Inc.

de Vries, H. A. 1987. In W. P. Morgan and S. E. Goldston (Eds.) **Exercise and Mental Health** (pp. 99-104). Washington, DC: Hemisphere Publishing.

Greist, J. H., M. H. Klein, R. R. Eischens, A. S. Gurman and W. P. Morgan. 1979. "Running as a treatment for depression." *Comprehensive Psychiatry*, 20, 41-54.

Karam, C. 1989. **A Practical Guide to Cardiac Rehabilitation**. Rockville, MD: Aspen Publishers, Inc.

Martinsen, E. W., A. Medhus and L. Sandvik. 1984. "The effect of aerobic exercise on depression: A controlled study." Unpublished manuscript.

Sime, W. E. 1987. "Exercise in the treatment and prevention of depression." In W. P. Morgan and S. E. Goddamn (Eds.) **Exercise and Mental Health** (pp. 145-152). Washington DC: Hemisphere Publishing.

Taylor, C. B., J. F. Sallis and R. Needle. 1985. "The relation of physical activity and exercise to mental health." *Public Health Reports*, 100, 195-202.

Gardening Program (Structured Task)
Program Protocol

I. Treatment Modality
Gardening Program (Structured Task)
II. Rationale
The symptoms of depression which may be improved by structured task activities include: psychomotor retardation or agitation, difficulty concentrating, diminished interest or pleasure and feelings of worthlessness. In addition, patients who have schizophrenic or psychotic disorders may be helped if they exhibit disorganized thoughts, speech and behaviors which make initiative and execution of tasks more difficult.
Wassman and Iso-Ahola (1985) found that participation in structured activity treatment programs is effective in reducing depressive symptomatology and can increase levels of active engagement with one's surroundings. Improved self-control and sociability were noted as outcomes in an experimental study where elderly patients were given bird feeders and instructed in their use and care (Banzinger and Roush, 1983). Shary and Iso-Ahola (1989) randomly assigned subjects to a horticulture group and observed significant improvement in perceived competence. A study by Russoniello (1991) found that mood states and biochemical changes were positively affected by the participation in three structured treatment activities of low, moderate and high energy levels. Finally, in regards to psychotic symptoms, Wong et al (1987), Wong et al (1983) and Liberman et al (1984) found significant reductions in hallucinatory speech, inappropriate laughter and bizarre behaviors when patients were engaged in structured recreational activities.

III. Referrals

Patients will be referred to the gardening program if they exhibit:

1. difficulty concentrating
2. diminished interest or pleasure
3. psychomotor retardation
4. feelings of worthlessness
5. psychotic symptoms of disorganized thoughts, speech or behaviors

IV. Risk Management

Patients will be screened for any contraindicating conditions including: skeletal injures, allergies, compromised skin integrity and pulmonary difficulties.

Patients who have psychotic disorders will be screened daily. When they are directable, they may be include in this program. When the psychosis is severely intrusive and the patient is not directable, s/he will be prohibited from the group in order to allow destimulation and to protect other patients.

Patients with photosensitivity due to medications will be provided with appropriate sun protection (e.g., sun tan lotion with an SPF factor of 30 or greater applied 30 minutes before an outdoor activity).

V. Criteria

Structure Criteria	Process Criteria	Outcome Criteria
The gardening program will be conducted for 60 minutes, three days a week in the garden area, weather permitting. In case of inclement weather and during the winter months, patients will complete activities in the indoor garden center.	The recreational therapist will assure that all patients are medically screened for the intervention and that the space is free of potential hazards.	
Modules will involve the patient in a series of tasks that may include:	The therapist will:	The patient will:
1. Cognitive — Care and maintenance of indoor foliage	1. Assist patients in problem solving and decision making regarding appropriate care of plants.	1. Identify and process complex problems utilizing positive decision making techniques.
2. Physical — Outdoor ground preparation, adaptive gardening techniques for various spaces and levels of ability, planting and maintaining outdoor gardens	2a. Assist patients in identifying viable options for personal involvement in gardening despite limitations. 2b. Instruct patients in the benefits of physical activity in a non-threatening environment.	2. Execute physical tasks according to his/her level of ability.
3. Social — Cooperative group planning and execution, nature crafts skill development	3a. Assist group in positive interactions among members. 3b. Instruct group in nature crafts.	3. Interact cooperatively with group members toward completion of tasks.

Structure Criteria	Process Criteria	Outcome Criteria
4. Psychological — Opportunities for success and demonstration of initiative	4. Structure activities with increasing levels of complexity.	4. Display more confidence in self and demonstrate initiative.

VI. Credentialling

The therapist will demonstrate knowledge of horticulture and group leadership techniques.

VII. Bibliography

Banzinger, G. and S. Rousch. 1983 "Nursing homes for the birds: A control-relevant intervention with bird feeders." *The Gerontologist*. 23, 527-531.

Coyle, C. P., W. B. Kinney, R. Riley, J. Shank (Eds.) 1991. **Benefits of Therapeutic Recreation: A Consensus View**. Ravensdale, WA: Idyll Arbor, Inc.

Liberman, R. P., F. J. Lillie, I. R. H. Falloon, E. J. Harpin, W. Hutchison and B. A. Stout. 1984. "Social skills training for relapsing schizophrenics: An experimental analysis." *Behavioral Modification*. 8, 155-179.

Russoniello, C. V. 1991. "An exploratory study of physiological and psychological changes in alcoholic patients after recreation therapy treatments." Paper presented at the Benefits of Therapeutic Recreation in Rehabilitation Conference, Lafayette Hill, PA.

Shary, J. and S. Iso-Ahola. 1989. "Effects of a control relevant intervention program on nursing home residents' perceived competence and self-esteem." *Therapeutic Recreation Journal*. 23, 7-16.

Wassman, K. B. and S. E. Iso-Ahola. 1985. "The relationship between recreation participation and depression in psychiatric patients." *Therapeutic Recreation Journal*. 19 (3), 63-70.

Wong, S. E., M. D. Terranova, L. Bowen and R Zarate. 1987. "Providing independent recreational activities to reduce stereotypic vocalization in chronic schizophrenics." *Journal of Applied Behavior Analysis*. 20, 77-81.

Wong, S. E., M. D. Terranova, B. D. Marshall, L. K. Banzett and R. P. Liberman. 1983. "Reducing bizarre stereotypic behavior in chronic psychiatric patients: Effects of supervised and independent recreational activities." Presented at the Ninth Annual Convention of the Association of Behavior Analysis, Milwaukee, WI.

Leisure Education Program
Program Protocol

I. Treatment Modality

Leisure Education Program

II. Rationale

Improvement of perceived well-being through participation in a leisure education program has been suggested by Skalko (1982). Significant improvement of perceived leisure competence with the use of a leisure education program was identified by Searle and Mahon (1991, 1993). Bullock and Howe (1991) found improvement in behavioral functioning, adjustment to disability, autonomy and quality of life after patients participated in a reintegration program utilizing leisure education.

III. Referrals

Patients are referred to this program who have been identified, through a comprehensive assessment, as having limitations or difficulties in one or more of the following areas:

1. leisure awareness
2. leisure attitude
3. leisure skills
4. social appropriateness
5. group interaction skills
6. sub-optimal recreation participation patterns

Patients who are not directable are contraindicated.

IV. Risk Management

When gross motor activities are used in this program, patients will be assessed beforehand for any possible contraindications.

V. Criteria

Structure Criteria	Process Criteria	Outcome Criteria
The leisure education program will be conducted for 60 minutes, three times a week in the group treatment room. Modules will address and further assess the following areas:	The recreational therapist will assure that all patients are medically screened for the intervention and that the space is free of potential hazards. The therapist will:	The patient will:
1. leisure awareness	1. Assist the patient in identifying his/her knowledge of leisure appropriate to future leisure needs.	1. Identify personal benefits of leisure involvement, leisure strengths and weaknesses, expectations and goals regarding leisure involvement.
2. leisure attitude	2. Assist the patient in identifying his/her behaviors and/or feelings toward leisure involvement.	2. Identify his/her disposition toward leisure and recreation and at least one additional way to direct future involvement.
3. leisure skills	3. Assist the patient in identifying his/her leisure skills and the potential for the acquisition of additional skills.	3. Inventory present leisure skills and express willingness to develop new ones.
4. social appropriateness	4. Assist the patient in identifying specific social behaviors which affect his/her ability to function effectively in leisure activities.	4. Display self-directed socially acceptable behaviors in regards to manners, personal hygiene and dress, courteousness and tolerance for others.

Structure Criteria	Process Criteria	Outcome Criteria
5. group interaction skills	5. Assist the patient in acquiring interaction skills to participate in various types of individual and/or group situations.	5. Interact cooperatively and competitively in socially acceptable ways.
6. recreation participation	6. Assist the patient in active participation in recreational activities.	6. Participate actively for the duration of the program without direct prompting from staff.
7. recreation resources	7. Assist the patient in identifying personal and community resources for use after discharge.	7. Develop a plan to utilize personal and community resources after discharge.

VI. Credentialling

The therapist will hold national certification as a therapeutic recreation specialist or hold a valid license as a recreational therapist.

VII. Bibliography

Bullock, C. C. and C. Z. Howe. 1991. "A model therapeutic recreation program for the reintegration of persons with disabilities in the community." *Therapeutic Recreation Journal*. 25 (1), 7-17.

Coyle, C. P., W. B. Kinney, R. Riley, J. Shank (Eds.) 1991. **Benefits of Therapeutic Recreation: A Consensus View**. Ravensdale, WA: Idyll Arbor, Inc.

Kloseck, M. and Lammers. 1989. "Leisure Competence Measure." (A cooperative research project between Parkwood Hospital, London, Ontario, Canada and Oklahoma State University, Oklahoma.)

Searle, M. S. and M. J. Mahon. 1991. "Leisure education in a day hospital: The effects on selected social-psychological variables among older adults." *Canadian Journal of Community Mental Health*. 10(2), 95-109.

Searle, M. S. and M. J. Mahon. 1993. "The effects of a leisure education program on selected social-psychological variables: A three month follow-up investigation." *Therapeutic Recreation Journal*, 27 (1), 9-21.

Skalko, T. K. 1982. "The effects of leisure education program on the perceived leisure well-being of psychiatrically impaired active army personnel." Unpublished doctoral dissertation. University of Maryland: College Park, MD.

Stress Management and Relaxation
Program Protocol

I. Treatment Modality

Stress Management and Relaxation

II. Rationale

While there are complex psychobiological causes of mental illness, it can be argued that cumulative stress or significant stressful events can precipitate or aggravate acute episodes of illness.

Matheny et al (1986) found social skills training, problem-solving, cognitive restructuring and relaxation training to be among the more effective treatments for stress related disorders. They suggest a treatment program that includes stress monitoring, marshaling resources (assertiveness training, confronting and dealing with issues), cognitive therapies and tension reduction (relaxation, meditation training, and exercise).

In a clinical trial, Carrigan et al (1980) compared subjects using three different modalities — medication, meditation and progressive muscle relaxation. After five months, they found the meditation group showed significantly more symptom reduction than other groups. In addition, subjects showed improvement on the SCL-90-R in every one of the symptom scales, including somatization, depression, anxiety, hostility (p <0.001 for each), interpersonal sensitivity, paranoid ideation, psychoticisms (p <0.01 for each) and obsessive-compulsive and phobic anxiety (p <0.05 for each).

III. Referrals

Patients will be referred to this program who have depressive disorders with/without personality disorders and who report significant stresses in their lives. It is helpful if patients have been introduced to the cognitive therapy process and cognitive distortions.

IV. Risk Management

Patients who are not indicated for this program include those with organic mental disturbances or who have acute episodes of psychosis. Several categories of patients deserve special consideration. Patients who have dissociative disorders may require medical authorization before beginning any meditation or relaxation techniques. Those who have been sexually abused may feel more vulnerable during relaxation and meditation activities. They may want to self-select out of this part of the program or engage in such activities apart from the group. Finally, patients who have active seizure disorders should have medical approval before starting relaxation/meditation.

V. Criteria

Structure Criteria	Process Criteria	Outcome Criteria
The Stress Management and Relaxation program will meet three days a week, for 60 minutes each. There will be three modules, each including a 40 minute psycho-educational component and a 20 minute experiential tension reduction part. Modules include:	The recreational therapist will assure that all patients are medically screened for the intervention and that the space is free of potential hazards. The therapist will:	The patient will:
1a. Stress monitoring	1a. Assist patients in identifying source of stress and the biopsychosocial symptoms of stress.	1a. Be able to identify symptoms for self-monitoring of stress.
1b. Tension reduction exercise	1b. Lead patients in appropriate tension reduction exercise.	1b. Perform appropriate tension reduction exercises.
2a. Marshaling resources	2a. Assist group in identifying helpful strategies for managing stress, including but not limited to: developing support systems, time management, use of play, setting priorities, being assertive. 2b. Refer patients to community resources or literature where they may learn further about these strategies.	2a. Be able to identify effective coping strategies for self-management. 2b. List appropriate resources for additional help after discharge.
2c. Progressive muscle relaxation	2c. Instruct patients in progressive muscle relaxation.	2c. Use proactive progressive muscle relaxation.

Structure Criteria	Process Criteria	Outcome Criteria
3a. Cognitive restructuring	3a. Lead discussion of cognitive responses to stress and appropriate rational responses.	3a. State a rational response to thoughts about stress.
3b. Mindfulness meditation	3b. Instruct patients in mindfulness meditation.	3b. Practice mindfulness meditation.

VI. Credentialling

The therapist will have demonstrated training and competence in stress management theory and relaxation training.

VII. Bibliography

Baldwin, B. 1985. **It's All In Your Head: Lifestyle Management Strategies for Busy People**. Wilmington, NC: Direction Dynamics.

Benson, H. 1975. **Relaxation Response**. New York: Avon Books.

Benson, H. and E. Stuart. 1992. **The Wellness Book: A Comprehensive Guide to Maintaining Health and Treating Stress-Related Illness**. New York: Birch Lane Press.

Benson, H., I. Kutz and J. Borysenko. 1985. "Meditation and Psychotherapy: a Rationale for the Integration of Dynamic Psychotherapy, the Relaxation Response and Mindfulness Meditation." *American Journal of Psychiatry*. 142 (1), 1-8.

Carrigan, P., G. H. Collinger, Jr., H. Benson, H. Robinson, L. W. Wood, P. M. Lehrer, R. L. Woolfolf and J. W. Cole. 1980. "The use of meditation — relaxation techniques for the management of stress in a working population." *Journal of Occupational Medicine*. 22 (4), 221-231.

Coyle, C. P., W. B. Kinney, R. Riley, J. Shank (Eds.) 1991. **Benefits of Therapeutic Recreation: A Consensus View**. Ravensdale, WA: Idyll Arbor, Inc.

Davis, M., E. Robbins Eshelman and M. McKay. 1995. **The Relaxation and Stress Reduction Workbook, Fourth Edition**. Oakland, CA: New Harbinger Publications.

de Vries, H. A. 1987. "Tension Reduction with Exercise." In Wm. P. Morgan and S. E. Goldston (Eds.) **Exercise and Mental Health**. Washington, DC: Hemisphere Publishing.

Matheny, K. S., D. W. Aycock, J. Pugh, W. L. Curlette, K. A. Silva Cannella. 1986. "Stress Coping: A Qualitative and Quantitative Synthesis and Implications for Treatment." *The Counseling Psychologist*. 14 (4), 499-549.

Friendship Development
Program Protocol

I. Treatment Modality

Friendship Development

II. Rationale

Patients with depressive disorders and personality disorders are at high risk for friendship disorders because social behaviors are often part of the symptomatology of mental illness. Turner (1981) and Leavy (1983) found an association between the absence of social supports and increased psychological stress. In an extensive review of the literature, Antonucci (1989) found evidence that a social support system is related to a variety of cost-effective outcomes, including a decrease in mental illness symptoms, a reduction in help-seeking behavior and a reduced need for hospitalization and shorter lengths of stay when admitted.

III. Referrals

Patients will be referred to the friendship development program who:

1. have difficulty initiating and sustaining social conversations
2. hold dysfunctional beliefs about the nature of friends and friendships
3. report a narrow field of social supports

Patients who are non-directable are contraindicated for this program.

It is presumed that patients have been introduced to the cognitive therapy process and have learned to use the daily mood log in other treatment groups.

IV. Risk Management

This program doesn't present organizational risk.

V. Criteria

Structure Criteria	Process Criteria	Outcome Criteria
The friendship development program will meet three times a week for sixty minutes. There are three modules in the program:	The therapist will:	The patient will:
1. Improve social skills	1a. Distribute literature and lead discussion about non-verbal communication, how to start a conversation and the importance of giving and receiving feedback. 1b. Assign role playing situations, process results with group. 1c. Assign homework.	1. Exhibit improved ability to initiate conversations, give and receive feedback and understand nonverbal communication cues.
2. Modifying dysfunctional beliefs	2a. Ask patients to identify thoughts they hold about the nature of friendship or about themselves or others in a friendship. 2b. Assist patients in the use of the daily mood log to reformat dysfunctional beliefs. 2c. Use advantages vs. disadvantages format to help patients weigh the advantages of holding onto dysfunctional beliefs. 2d. Assign homework.	2. Relate functional beliefs about the nature of friends and friendships.

Structure Criteria	Process Criteria	Outcome Criteria
3. Developing a social support system	3a. Ask patients to identify lapsed social supports from the past they can re-establish. 3b. Ask patients to identify appropriate and safe places and resources where they can make friends. 3c. Use problem-solving techniques with patients to overcome external barriers to achieving friends (e.g., transportation). 3d. Assign homework.	3. Identify a plan to seek social supports in the community

VI. Credentialling

Therapists must demonstrate knowledge and skill in the use of cognitive therapy techniques.

VII. Bibliography

Antonucci, T. C. 1989. "Social Support Influences on the Disease Process." In L. Carstensen and J. Neale (Eds.). **Mechanisms of Psychological Influence on Physical Health**. (pp. 23-41). New York: Plenum Press.

Burns, D. D. 1989. **The Feeling Good Handbook**. New York: Wm. Morrow & Company, Inc.

Gabor, D. 1983. **How to Start a Conversation and Make Friends**. New York: Simon and Schuster.

Leavy, R. L. 1983. "Social Support and Psychological Disorder." *Journal of Community Psychology*, 11, 3-21.

Turner, R. J. 1981. "Social Support as a Contingency in Psychological Well-Being." *Journal of Health and Social Behavior*. 22, 357-367.

Young, J. T. 1986. "A Cognitive-Behavioral Approach to Friendship Disorders." In V. J. Derlego and B. A. Winstead. **Friendship in Social Interaction**. (pp. 247-276). New York: Springer-Verlag.

Zimbardo, P. 1977. **Shyness: What It Is. What to Do About It**. Reading, MA: Wesley Publishing Company.

Treatment Plans

A treatment plan is the written description of the specific treatment and service that the individual patient is to receive. Treatment plans, also called care plans, are written in behavioral terms and need to be measurable (what, when, how much, by whom) and are modified as the patient's status changes.

Although the appearance of treatment plans vary widely from one hospital setting to another, the content (long-term and short-term goals, behavioral objective and discharge plans) is fairly consistent. Some departments are excellent at completing truly interdisciplinary or integrated treatment plans. Despite requirements from regulatory agencies, some programs persist with variations of multidisciplinary plans that allow each discipline to formulate its own treatment goals for the patient.

Individualized treatment planning is a critical step in the therapeutic process. In psychiatric settings, the process of treatment planning often follows an interdisciplinary, problem-centered model. This problem-centered approach is recommended by the Joint Commission on Health Care Organizations which accredits psychiatric programs. It has been used as the model for treatment planning by state departments of mental health which license psychiatric beds and programs.

The problem-centered approach as it is used in recreational therapy includes the following steps:

1. Assessment of the patent's psychosocial, physical and leisure functioning.

2. Identification of the patient's strengths and weaknesses.

3. Determination of therapeutic goal(s) or outcome(s), that the patient can realistically achieve as a result of treatment.

4. Objectives or steps that are written in behavioral and measurable terms that the patient must meet in order to accomplish the goal.

5. Intervention strategies that staff will use to assist the patient in accomplishing the behavioral objective.

6. A review date when the plan for the patient will be evaluated and either continued, revised or discontinued.

The treatment plans in this book are offered to recreational therapists and students as guidelines to problem-centered individualized treatment planning.

This collection of goals, behavioral objectives and interventions, based on identified problems of the patient, are intended for instructional use and to aid the process of standardization. By sharing common interventions, our field will be able to accumulate information which will help further our measurement of the efficacy of our services.

These treatment plans, of course, are not all-inclusive. There are other problems that psychiatric patients present to us and other goals and objectives that we may identify. As the line between "professional territory" continues to blur, we may also find that the types of interventions that we direct may have been historically thought of as belonging to another field. (Or a professional with different training may help implement some of the services historically thought of as belonging only to recreational therapy.)

While these sample treatment plans were written based on our practice with psychiatric patients, the therapist may find that many of them may be used with patients who have rehabilitation or general medicine diagnoses also.

To use these treatment plans, the therapist will first need to determine the type of problem to be addressed. This portion of the book has the treatment care plans divided into five sections: behavioral, affective, cognitive, physical and leisure. The first page of each section has a master list of the problems for the section. Using the master list of problem-oriented plans, the therapist can locate the specific treatment plan that s/he wants to review. The therapist will want to review the written treatment plan and then make modifications to that plan to make it more specific to each patient's treatment needs.

Creating original and descriptive documentation on each patient's status for any aspect of treatment can be challenging. Below the treatment plan you will find a short list of terms which relate to the treatment plan on that page. You can use these words to help create a more descriptive chart note or to help modify the treatment plan to match the needs of your patient.

The thesaurus is organized into two word lists: negative terms and positive/neutral terms. These words may be used to describe the range of patient behaviors as you create individualized treatment plans and later report on the patient's progress.

Behavioral Domain

1. Resistance to Treatment
2. Poor Time Management
3. Poor Impulse Control — Violating Others Personal Space
4. Poor Impulse Control — Wandering
5. Extreme Agitation
6. Poor Personal Hygiene
7. Anxious Behavior
8. Low Tolerance for Interaction
9. Loud Voice
10. Intrusiveness
11. Too Many Demands
12. Staff Splitting, Manipulation
13. Passivity, Self Isolation
14. Superficiality, Difficulty Expressing Feelings
15. Obnoxiousness, Offensive Behavior
16. Paranoia, Distrust
17. Overt Hostility
18. Pressured Speech, Hyper Talkativeness
19. Somaticization
20. Hopelessness
21. Obsessive-Compulsive Behavior
22. Difficulty Sleeping

Resistance to Treatment

Behavioral Domain

Problem	Goal	Objective	Intervention
Resistance to treatment	To accept treatment and make progress toward recovery.	Patient will be able to explain the purpose of this therapy.	Compromise about schedule to start. Make brief daily visits to increase rapport.
		Patient will negotiate and agree to a limited schedule to begin with.	Establish a verbal/written agreement for attendance.
		Patient will attend 50% (75%, 100%) of scheduled groups this week.	Ask patient to identify goals for admission and how recreation therapy can help meet those goals.
		Patient will respond to activity topic 1 (2, 3) times in 50% (75%, 100%) of treatment groups daily.	Remind patient that s/he can help in getting well by taking an interest in activities.
		Patient will choose 1 (2, 3) activities each day in his/her free time.	Review content of group beforehand.
			Remind about groups beforehand.
			Draw patient into unit activities in free time, introduce to peers to help establish rapport.

Negative Terms To Aid Documentation

aloof	egocentric	menacing	recalcitrant	unacceptable
avoids routine	evasive	mocking	refuses	uncooperative
breaks rules	immobile	non-compliant	reluctant	unfriendly
challenging	immovable	opinionated	resistant	willful
condescending	intimidating	oppositional	territorial	
confrontive	intractable	questions authority	tests limits	
derogatory	manipulative	rebellious	testy	

Positive/Neutral Terms To Aid Documentation

active	cooperative	inclined	redirectable	willing
agreeable	enthusiastic	invested	reliable	
compliant	helpful	motivated	responsive	

Poor Time Management

Behavioral Domain

Problem	Goal	Objective	Intervention
Poor time management	To increase time management skills.	Patient will plan a daily schedule on his/her own 50% (75%, 100%) of the time. Patient will review his/her schedule for the day before breakfast and again after lunch to assist with managing his/her time. Patient will arrive on time for group 50% (75%, 100%) of the time.	Help patient develop a written daily schedule that is easy for him/her to use. It is best if the system can be used after discharge also. Review patient's schedule of activities; ask patient if there are any questions about the groups. Talk with patient about the effect of his/her lateness on the group and patient's responsibility to follow schedule. Help patient identify time management techniques to get organized.

Negative Terms to Aid Documentation

control	disoriented	loiter	procrastinate	underestimate time needed
creates unnecessary work	habitual tardiness	overworked	stall	watches clock
dawdle	late	postpone	too busy	

Positive/Neutral Terms To Aid Documentation

direction	handle	on time	punctual	self-directed
duration	industrious	organized	regulate	timely
early	interval	prompt	schedule	well-timed

Poor Impulse Control — Violating Other's Space
Behavioral Domain

Problem	Goal	Objective	Intervention
Poor impulse control, i.e., turning stereo up whenever s/he wants to	To improve impulse control.	Patient will not turn volume up during activity 50% (75%, 100%) of the time. Patient will ask others before doing something that intrudes on their space with 0 (1, 2) errors in a 24 hour period.	Provide the patient with a clear guideline of what is too loud by using the numbers on the volume control or other, similar means. Offer to give patient the opportunity to play loud music later at a convenient time and location. Ask patient to respect other patients in the room. Draw patient into another activity to refocus attention.

Negative Terms to Aid Documentation

aggressive	controlling	impetuous	short fuse	unpredictable
annoying	distractible	lashes out	sudden thought	urge
attention seeking	excitable	losing control	unawares	
belligerent	hostile	rash	uninhibited	

Positive/Neutral Terms To Aid Documentation

aware of boundaries	cooperative	redirectable	responsive	sociable
calm	mannerly	respectful	sensitive	tactful

Treatment Plans

Poor Impulse Control — Wandering

Behavioral Domain

Problem	Goal	Objective	Intervention
Poor impulse control, i.e., walking away from group	To improve impulse control. To decrease wandering.	Patient will participate in activity 10 (20, 30) minutes increasing participation time 5 minutes per group. Patient will stand up but remain with activity 50% (75%, 100%) of the time. Patient will take 5 minutes break, then return to activity 50% (75%, 100%) of the time. Patient will ask permission before leaving the group 50% (75%, 100%) of the time.	Ask patient to try to remain another 5 (10, 15 minutes). Call patient by name to draw patient's attention back to activity. Allow patient to take a short stretch if necessary. Use gross motor activity to release anxious tension.

Negative Terms to Aid Documentation

abrupt	drift	meander	short attention span	wander
anxious	elope	over-stimulated	stray
AWOL	fidgety	ramble	uncomfortable
compelled	impulsive	roam	uncomfortable in groups

Positive/Neutral Terms To Aid Documentation

attention span	concentration	patient	settled	tolerant
attentive	cooperative	planted	stationary
comfortable	focused	redirectable	stays with group

Extreme Agitation

Behavioral Domain

Problem	Goal	Objective	Intervention
Extreme agitation	To decrease agitation.	Patient will need only 1 (2, 3) cues from staff to go to his/her room to decrease stimulation and manage agitation.	Speak calmly to patient.
			Allow patient to miss group at this time.
		Patient will develop 2 (4, 6) strategies to reduce agitation.	Advise nursing staff on patient's condition.
		Patient will recognize beginning of agitation and use strategies to reduce agitation 50% (75%, 100%) of the time.	When agitation is beginning, ask patient if s/he needs to use one of his/her agitation-reducing strategies.

Negative Terms to Aid Documentation

aggressive	exaggerated	inappropriate anger	provoked	stirred up
annoyed	excessive animation	irritated	rapid	tantrum-like
destructive	frantic	nervous	restless	tense
disturbed	hurried	over-responsive	run-together	worried
easily excitable	hyperactive	pace/cadence too fast	squirming	

Positive/Neutral Terms To Aid Documentation

calm	even-tempered	not rushed	relaxed	steady
cooperative	not excitable	quiet	stable	

Treatment Plans

Poor Personal Hygiene

Behavioral Domain

Problem	Goal	Objective	Intervention
Poor personal hygiene	To improve self-care skills.	Patient will be dressed, groomed, wearing shoes prior to group 50% (75%, 100%) of the time.	Use time management strategies. Suggest to patient that s/he get up a little earlier in the morning to be ready on time, suggest bringing an alarm clock from home.
		Patient will correct self-care deficiency with one (two, three) verbal reminders.	Provide the patient with a written or pictorial guide to appropriate dressing to be used as a check list by the patient prior to the activity.
		Patient will be able to identify proper self-care regimen (can be broken down into individual tasks — bathing, washing hair, brushing teeth, etc.).	Remind patient one-half hour before group to review check list.
		Patient will demonstrate ability to clean his/her own clothes.	Discuss personal appearance as an issue of pride and self-esteem.
			Reinforce rule about appropriate dress and appearance for groups.

Negative Terms to Aid Documentation

baggy	grungy	offensive body order	rumpled	tobacco-stained
clean but worn	heavy makeup	oily	scraggly hair	unbuttoned
disheveled	ill-fitting	out of shape	seductive appearance	unkempt
dress to offend	indicating indifference	overdressed	sloppy	unshaven
eccentric	ineffective deodorant	overlong nails	slovenly	untidy
excessive perfume	matted hair	pale	smelly	unzipped
flashy	messy	poor self care	soiled	wrong size
food stained	neglected appearance	poor taste	tight-fitting	

Positive/Neutral Terms To Aid Documentation

appropriate makeup	clean	fresh breath	neat	tidy
careful	clean but worn	good taste	self image	well groomed
carefully disordered	fashionable	meticulous	shaved	

Anxious Behavior

Behavioral Domain

Problem	Goal	Objective	Intervention
Anxious behaviors (fidgeting, difficulty staying in chair, tapping, purposeless actions)	To decrease anxious behaviors.	Patient will tolerate activity 5 (10, 15) minutes without demonstrating anxious behavior 50% (75%, 100%) of the time.	Ask patient to try activity for a certain amount of time, agree to allow patient to leave the activity after the agreed upon time if s/he wishes.
		Patient will stop anxious behavior with 1 (2, 3) reminders.	Use gross motor activities to relieve tension, i.e., exercise, sports, games.
		Patient will stop behavior with one signal cue from therapist 50% (75%, 100%) of the time.	Identify a signal cue to use with patient when the behavior is exhibited.
			Provide patient with an alternative anxious behavior that is less distracting to the group if a multiple-step intervention is necessary (e.g., a seven inch long cloth ribbon to fidget with instead of tapping a pencil).

Negative Terms to Aid Documentation

bothered	fidgeting	oversensitive	repetitive movements	tightness in chest
churning stomach	inhibited movements	overstimulated	restlessness	troubled
clutching hands	insecure	pacing	self-hugging	uncertain
concerned	internal tension	panicked	shuffles feet	uneasy
dry mouth	moistens lips	perturbed	sitting on edge of chair	vulnerable
excessive perspiration	nail biting	queasiness	sweaty palms	worried look
fearful	nervous	racing heartbeat	tapping	

Positive/Neutral Terms To Aid Documentation

amenable to suggestions	collected	patient	poised	relaxed
at ease	composed	peaceful	quiet	
calm	confident	placid	redirectable	

Low Tolerance for Interaction

Behavioral Domain

Problem	Goal	Objective	Intervention
Low tolerance for interaction	To increase toleration for interaction.	Patient will interact with therapist 5 (10, 15) minutes 1 (2, 3) times per day.	1:1 approach. Use non-threatening matter-of-fact approach. Use parallel activities or activities that do not require a lot of talking.
		Patient will interact in group setting 10 (20, 30) minutes 1 (2, 3) times per day.	Allow patient to play or sit alone at first, or in parallel activities.
		Patient will initiate an interaction with another person 1 (2, 3) times per day.	Allow for attendance without participation.
			As tolerance improves, pair patient with a peer or staff.
			Gradually draw patient into small group cooperative activities.
			Give significant time and positive feedback for interactions initiated by the patient.

Negative Terms to Aid Documentation

avoidance of others	guarded	negativistic	resistive	unable to abide
disorganized	insecure	over-stimulated	self-doubting	unable to bear
distracted	intimidated	poor rapport-building skill	shy	unsure
distrusts own ability	isolates self	reluctant	subtle hostility	withdraws
doesn't know what to say	minimal interaction	remote	territorial	

Positive/Neutral Terms To Aid Documentation

agreeable	caring	engaging	initiates interactions	sympathetic
amicable	empathetic	friendly	reciprocal	
builds rapport	endurance	good social skills	socializes	

Loud Voice
Behavioral Domain

Problem	Goal	Objective	Intervention
Loud voice	To speak in normal tone of voice.	Patient will use normal tone of voice after 1 (2, 3) reminders from staff.	Remind patient to calm down and speak slowly in normal tone of voice.
		Patient will identify other ways to get appropriate attention besides using a loud voice.	Help the patient find other ways to get attention besides using a loud voice.
		Patient will succeed in getting attention with alternate method at least 50% (75%, 100%) of the time.	Establish signal cue with patient to use when behavior is exhibited.
		Patient will modify loud voice behavior with just 1 (2, 3) cues required from the therapist in a 30 (60) minute activity.	

Negative Terms to Aid Documentation

boisterous	harsh	noisy	resounding	shrill
controlling	high pitched	odd intonation	roaring	thunderous
excessive	labile	overbearing	screaming	

Positive/Neutral Terms To Aid Documentation

adequate	composed	cool-headed	normal	warm
calm	conversational tone	measured	pleasant	well modulated

Treatment Plans

79

Intrusiveness
Behavioral Domain

Problem	Goal	Objective	Intervention
Intrusiveness	To improve social skills.	Patient will interrupt conversation less than 6 (5, 3, 1) times per 30 minute period.	Stop activity/conversation so that patient knows s/he has interrupted.
		Patient will respond to cueing 50% (75%, 100%) of attempts.	Let patient know s/he will have an opportunity to speak.
		Patient will keep the thought until s/he has a chance to speak 50% (75%, 100%) of the time.	Establish a signal cue to use with patient when behavior is exhibited.
			Let patient know before group what is expected from patient and ask patient to monitor his/her own intrusiveness.
			Tell the patient that s/he has the ability to control his/her behavior and will be asked to leave if unable to do so.

Negative Terms to Aid Documentation

annoying	ignores boundaries	interrupts	needy
break in	imprudent	intrude	over step
disruptive	impulsive	irritating	repetitive violation
encroaching	interfering	manipulative	resistant to social rules

Positive/Neutral Terms To Aid Documentation

ability to wait	mature	polite	takes turns
cooperative	patient	respects boundaries	tolerant

Too Many Demands

Behavioral Domain

Problem	Goal	Objective	Intervention
Too many demands	To increase appropriate assertive social skills.	Patient will maintain control and wait until staff is able to assist him/her in 50% (75%, 100%) of episodes.	Tell patient s/he has the right to good care but that staff are limited and unable to respond to his/her needs immediately.
		Patient will organize requests or demands in order of importance so that the most important demands are dealt with first 50% (75%, 100%) of the time.	Set aside a time that is more convenient to meet with patient about his/her demands or needs.
			Assist patient in learning how to prioritize needs and how to identify the actual degree of urgency of each need.
		Patient will make requests or demands known in writing 50% (75%, 100%) of the time.	Ask patient to submit request or demands in writing.

Negative Terms to Aid Documentation

arrogant	demanding of favors	heedless of others needs	needy	thoughtless
contemptuous	demanding of sympathy	insatiable needs	requiring	uses others
controlling	entitled	insistent	selfish	wanting
demanding	exploitative	intimidating	socially insensitive	
demanding of affection	fragile self-esteem	manipulative	somatic	

Positive/Neutral Terms To Aid Documentation

assertive	compliant	flexible	patient	yielding
calm	compromises	giving	waits for turn	

Treatment Plans

81

Manipulation
Behavioral Domain

Problem	Goal	Objective	Intervention
Staff splitting; manipulation	To eliminate staff splitting.	Patient will not play one staff against another, i.e., asking multiple staff for the same things, going to another staff person if not satisfied with the response from the first 50% (75%, 100%) of the time.	Redirect patient back to the primary nurse or therapist to resolve the issue. Do not try to negotiate patient's conflicts with other staff.
		Patient will appropriately appeal decisions that s/he doesn't like by informing the second staff person of the history of the request 50% (75%, 100%) of the time.	Instruct the patient in basic rules associated with conflict resolution. Display conflict resolution rules in either written or pictorial form. Refer the patient to these as needed.
		Patient will demonstrate appropriate conflict resolution skills when feeling "wronged" by a staff person or another patient with no (1, 2, 3) errors in a 24 hour period.	

Negative Terms to Aid Documentation

conning	evasive	opportunistic	unethical
controlling	Machiavellian	predatory	unprincipled
deceitful	maneuvering	self-serving actions	unscrupulous
dishonest	manipulative	testing limits	using

Positive/Neutral Terms To Aid Documentation

accepting	cooperative	honest	redirectable	word play
assertive	engaging	rational	socially capable	socially effective

Passivity
Behavioral Domain

Problem	Goal	Objective	Intervention
Passivity, self isolating	To increase interaction with environment.	Patient will complete an individual activity which is at least 10 (20, 30) minutes in length by (date).	Structure non-threatening fun activities to increase patient's comfort level in socializing.
	To increase social interactions.	Patient will initiate verbal interaction 2 (3, 5) times in each group.	Use social skills activities to promote interaction, i.e., paired activities, small group discussion.
		Patient will appropriately assert his/her preferences in group activities by (date).	Ask patient to report his/her progress after each group so that patient is actively working towards his/her goal.
		Patient will select 1 (2, 3) activities to participate in for at least 10 (20, 30) minutes each day.	Teach assertion skills. Let patient know that each person's opinion is valued. Confront non-assertive behavior.
		Patient will correctly evaluate his/her contribution to group discussions 50% (75%, 100%) of the time.	Encourage positive peer pressure.
		Patient will respond appropriately to pet therapy 50% (75%, 100%) of the time.	Use pet therapy.

Negative Terms to Aid Documentation

absent	docile	insecure	secludes self	uninvolved
aloof	inactive	remote	shallow	unresponsive
detached	inert	retreat	submissive	

Positive/Neutral Terms To Aid Documentation

active	alert	attentive	enthusiastic	present
agreeable	assertive	eager	motivated	social

Treatment Plans

Superficiality
Behavioral Domain

Problem	Goal	Objective	Intervention
Superficiality, difficulty expressing feelings	To verbalize feelings.	Patient will respond to topic when requested 50% (75%, 100%) of time in groups.	Use expressive media — music, art, writing.
			Use social skills techniques, including dyads or small group discussion.
		Patient will initiate 1 (2, 3) comments relative to topic in 50% (75%, 100%) of groups.	Be supportive, non-judgmental.
			Let patient know it is safe to share feelings.
		After groups, patient will identify his/her response to group activity when requested by therapist.	Encourage patient to talk about self, experiences, strengths.
		Patient will share personal information 1 (2, 3) times per day.	Confront superficial statements or joking which is inappropriate to content of discussion or activity.
		Patient will respond appropriately to shared information from others 50% (75%, 100%) of the time.	Discuss expectations regarding communicating feelings.
		Patient will be able to identify 4 (6, 8) different feelings correctly when asked by staff 3 out of 4 (4 out of 4) times in a 24 hour period.	Have posters which depict different feelings on the unit. Talk about these with patient.
			Use therapeutic board games which address feeling identification.

Negative Terms to Aid Documentation

bland	detached	little variation	restricted	uninvolved
consistent	fake	masked	shallow	unresponsive
constrained	flat	muted	simple	vacant stare
cursory	indirect	not spontaneous	tangential	withdrawn
denial	inexpressive	passive	unchanging	

Positive/Neutral Terms To Aid Documentation

active	expressive	involved	sincere	verbal
communicative	in touch	open	spontaneous	
encouragable	initiating	simple	tie words to feelings	

Obnoxiousness, Offensive Behavior

Behavioral Domain

Problem	Goal	Objective	Intervention
Obnoxious, offensive behavior	To develop socially appropriate behavior that is not offensive or intrusive to others.	Patient will alter offensive behavior with 1 (2, 3) requests from therapist.	Give feedback about how his/her behavior affects the group.
		Patient will explain 1 (2, 3) ways his/her obnoxious behavior is detrimental to others.	Clearly define behaviors that aren't allowed and let patient know the consequences. Follow through with consequences.
		Patient will use appropriate ways to get attention 50% (75%, 100%) of the time.	Ask patient what other ways s/he can get attention from the group.
		Patient will demonstrate offensive behavior less than 2 (3, 5) times during each 60 minute activity.	Give patient positive reinforcement for socially appropriate behavior.
			Teach patient relaxation techniques.
		Patient will be able to demonstrate 1 (2, 3) new, socially appropriate behaviors each day.	Offer patient instruction in socially appropriate behaviors.

Negative Terms to Aid Documentation

abusive	frequent lying behavior	irresponsible	pandering	suggestive
bad taste	harasses	lascivious	predatory	unbecoming
cavalier attitude	humiliating	lewd	raw	uncivil
clownish	immodesty	lurid	rejects obligations	undignified
coarse	impolite	malicious	repugnant	unpleasant
controlling	improper	manipulative	repulsive	uses guilt as leverage
disrespectful	impulsive	nasty	risqué	vile
dominating	inappropriate	off-color	ruthless	violates social codes
financial irresponsibility	infringes on others	offensive	shameless	vulgar
foul-mouthed	intimidating	outlandish	socially destructive	

Positive/Neutral Terms To Aid Documentation

accessible	dignified	mannerly	relaxed
compassionate	friendly	mature	respectful
cooperative	kind	polite	social

Paranoia, Distrust
Behavioral Domain

Problem	Goal	Objective	Intervention
Paranoia, distrust	To increase level of trust.	Patient will participate in 1 (2, 3) trust building group activities by (date).	Use frequent, brief 1:1 contact.
			Listen to patient, don't get into power struggles with patient.
		Patient will participate in 1 (2, 3) parallel group activity by (date).	Use matter-of-fact approach, not demands.
		Patient will reduce personal space needed for comfort to 5 (3, 2) feet by (date).	Offer activities for patient's choice.
		Patient will demonstrate the validity of his/her feelings by identifying feeling, discussing impression of feeling with therapist, then taking action on feeling 1 (2, 3) times in a day.	Give patient wider personal space margin.
			Encourage attendance without participation from patient.
		Patient will identify for therapist 1 (2, 3) situations where another person was behaving respectfully toward patient during a day.	Instruct patient in the skills required to determine the trustworthiness of others.
		Patient will identify 1 (2, 3) aspects of trustworthy behavior by (date).	

Negative Terms to Aid Documentation

apprehension	disbelieve	fretful	panicked	worried look
avoidance behaviors	doubt	misgiving	unbelieving	

Positive/Neutral Terms To Aid Documentation

able to establish rapport	credible	rational	trusting
accepting	mutually respectful	reliable	validity of perception
believable	plausible	sure	

Treatment Plans

Overt Hostility
Behavioral Domain

Problem	Goal	Objective	Intervention
Overt hostility, angry outburst, throwing things, threat to harm self or others	To regain control of impulses.	Patient will regain control, will be able to discuss angry feelings without loud, aggressive outbursts 50% (75%, 100%) of the time.	Give patient space and distance. Remain calm. Let patient know s/he can ventilate anger in a socially acceptable manner. Do not become defensive or get involved in power struggle with patient. Ask patient how s/he can better deal with anger.
		Patient will identify 1 (2, 3) positive ways to express anger by (date).	Let patient know what the consequences are of continuing overtly hostile or aggressive behavior. Call for additional staff assistance and follow through with procedures to manage aggressive outbursts.
		Patient will not cause damage to objects around him/her in anger by (date).	Encourage use of a journal as a way to vent anger.
		Patient will not cause harm to people around him/her in anger by (date).	Provide appropriate gross motor activities.
			Help patient identify triggers for overt hostility.
			Discuss with patient the degree to which anger is based on faulty reasoning.

Negative Terms to Aid Documentation

abrupt	displeasure	homicidal ideation	rash	takes offense
animosity	embitterment	impetuous	reckless	testy
aroused	exacerbating	indignation	repay	threatening
assaultive	exchange blows/words	lashes out	retaliating	unforgiving
bitter	explosive	look daggers	retributive	vengeful
boiling with rage	faulty reasoning	loses control	revenge	vindictive
bothered	flare-up	miffed	sardonic	worked up
bridled	fume	offensive	self-injurious behavior	wrath
combative	glower	over-stimulated	self-mutilating	
dangerous	grudge	provoke	sullen	
destructive	heated	rage	take exception	

Positive/Neutral Terms To Aid Documentation

conscientious	dignified	in control	mature	respectful
cooperative	hopeful	mannerly	redirectable	

Behavioral Health Protocols

Talkativeness

Behavioral Domain

Problem	Goal	Objective	Intervention
Pressured speech, hyper talkativeness	To speak at normal pace.	Patient will slow down speech when directed, requiring just 1 (2, 3) cues.	Provide feedback to patient, ask him/her to calm down and repeat what s/he has said.
		Patient will talk in normal pace so that others can easily comprehend 50% (75%, 100%) of the time.	Tell patient that s/he is talking non-stop.
			Suggest time out if too stimulated by activity.
		Patient will recognize when situation leads to pressured speech and use appropriate methods to reduce pressured speech 50% (75%, 100%) of the time (e.g., "I need to take a deep breath.").	Use audio tapes or videotapes to show behavior to patient.
			Work with patient on developing a cadence when talking.
			Provide patient with guidelines on good communication/listening skills in writing or pictorial format. Review with patient as needed.

Negative Terms to Aid Documentation

accelerated	diction	headlong	pronounce	stuttering
babble	enunciation	hyper-verbal	quickly	talkative
banter	excessive detail	inflection	rapidly	tempo
brisk	expansive	long-winded	rehearsed	unintelligible
careless	expressed	loquacity	rhetoric	utter
chant	gabby	monologue	run-together	verbose
chattering	gush	non-stop	rush	voicing an opinion
dialogue	hasty	pace	slurring	wordy

Positive/Neutral Terms To Aid Documentation

articulation	emphatic	measured	rhetoric	well modulated
dialog	enunciation	pace	tempo	
diction	inflection	pronounce	voicing an opinion	

Somatic Complaints
Behavioral Domain

Problem	Goal	Objective	Intervention
Somaticizing	To decrease somatic complaints.	Patient will concentrate on activity 15 (30, 60) minutes without somatic complaints.	Let patient know s/he can participate at his/her own pace, that there are many activities, resources, roles available to him/her within the structure of the activity.
		Patient will prioritize somatic complaints into ones that need to be dealt with immediately and ones that can wait by (date).	Don't reinforce somatic complaints with discussion.
		Patient will use list of prioritized complaints appropriately 50% (75%, 100%) of the time.	Validate patient's feelings by listening, then redirect patient's attention back to activity.
		Patient will choose level of activity which does not cause somatic complaints 50% (75%, 100%) of the time.	Use mater-of-fact approach.
			Refer patient with somatic complaints back to nurse or physician.

Negative Terms to Aid Documentation

affliction	excessive thoughts	inattentive	morbid thoughts	self-centeredness
ailment	grumbly	limited attention due to	obsession	sickness
distractible	hypochondria	low attending skills	perception	symptom
dominates thinking	illness	malady	preoccupied	whiny

Positive/Neutral Terms To Aid Documentation

authentic	genuine	illness	realistic
directable	healthy	perception	symptom
factual	honest	rational	validation

Hopelessness
Behavioral Domain

Problem	Goal	Objective	Intervention
Hopelessness	To have hope for recovery.	Patient will continue use of treatment program, will attend 50% (75%, 100%) scheduled groups per day.	Remind patient that there are no miracles, that recovery takes time and that staff will continue to work with him/her to get well.
		Patient will set personal goal for each day and report on progress.	Ask patient to set personal daily goal and identify steps needed to meet this goal. Ask patient to report on progress daily.
		Patient will complete task by (date).	Ask patient to consider what alternatives may help at this point.
		Patient will suggest at least 1 (2, 3) appropriate alternative activities each day and choose the alternative that seems the most desirable.	Use success-oriented activities.

Negative Terms to Aid Documentation

comfort	discouraged	inconsolable	submissive	yield to despair
confidence	disheartened	pessimistic	surrender	
despair	dismay	quitting	unrealistic expectations	
despondency	give up	ruined	useless	

Positive/Neutral Terms To Aid Documentation

assured	future-oriented	motivated	realistic
comforted	goal oriented	optimistic	security
enthusiastic	hopeful	positive	

Treatment Plans

95

Obsessive-Compulsive
Behavioral Domain

Problem	Goal	Objective	Intervention
Obsessive-compulsive behavior	To increase ability to function in activities.	Patient will participate in detail-oriented activity (e.g., folding napkins for a party table) which has a clear end point and stop when the activity is completed by (date).	Ask patient what s/he feels out of control about and discuss ways of resuming control of impulses through recreation participation.
		Patient will participate in activity 15 (30, 45) minutes with 0 (1, 2) incidents of identified obsessive or compulsive behavior which interfere with activity performance.	Decrease emphasis on competition and product completion. Emphasize the pleasure in the process. Focus attention on activities to decrease preoccupation with rituals. Redirect or distract patient from obsessive-compulsive behavior.

Negative Terms to Aid Documentation

concern over body parts	highly regulated	repetitive themes
controlling	hoarding	ritual behavior
elaborate planning	intense	ruminating
excessive cleaning	meticulous	socially demanding
excessively careful	over attention to detail	solemn
perfectionistic		
poor time management		
rechecking		
repetitive		
repetitive sequencing		
		work orientation

Positive/Neutral Terms To Aid Documentation

coping	process-oriented
rational	relaxed

Difficulty Sleeping
Behavioral Domain

Problem	Goal	Objective	Intervention
Difficulty sleeping	To get sufficient sleep at night.	Patient will sleep 6-8 hours a night.	Instruct patient in relaxation techniques to help sleep.
		Patient will use relaxation tape or other intervention such as exercise to help him/her sleep each night.	Furnish tapes and recorder to fall asleep with.
		Patient will get up at appropriate time each day.	Encourage patient to get up at regular time in the morning, maintain an active daily schedule and eliminate napping.
		Patient will use of relaxation tapes or interventions each day.	Encourage gross motor exercise up to 2 hours prior to bedtime.
		Patient will not nap during the day.	Discourage sugar or high caffeine intake after 6:00 p.m.
		Patient will drink 0 (1, 2) caffeine drinks each day.	

Negative Terms to Aid Documentation

aroused	incontinence	missing bed partner	reversal of sleep cycle	stimulants
being away from own bed	insomnia	night terrors	sleep deprivation	vivid dreams
cat naps	interrupted sleep	nightmares	sleep disruptions due to	wakefulness
chronic fatigue	inuresis	poor sleep environment	sleep disturbance	wide-awake
difficulty falling asleep	irregular bedtime	racing thoughts	sleepless	
early waking pattern	lethargy	restless sleep	snoring	

Positive/Neutral Terms To Aid Documentation

calm	energized	quiet	sleep-inducing	unhurried
drowsiness	placid	relaxed	total sleep time	well rested

Treatment Plans

Affective Domain

1. Anhedonia
2. Flat Affect
3. Inappropriate Laughter
4. Overly Bright Affect
5. Lability
6. Low Self-Esteem

Behavioral Health Protocols

Anhedonia
Affective Domain

Problem	Goal	Objective	Intervention
Anhedonia (no enjoyment in activities)	To increase enjoyment in activities.	Patient will choose an activity of interest and participate 15 (30, 45) minutes each day.	Discuss patient's responses to activities, benefits derived.
			Schedule patient for treatment activities.
		Patient will identify 2 (4, 6) activities enjoyed in past and identify what was enjoyable about them by (date).	Explore leisure attitudes, values and expectations learned at home.
		Patient will identify his/her barriers to enjoyment.	Explore more useful leisure attitudes, values and expectations to increase life satisfaction and stress management.
		Patient will participate in physical exercise for 15 (30, 60) minutes each day.	Use humor to stimulate positive response.
			Use either the Leisure Diagnostic Battery — Perceived Freedom Scale or the Leisure Satisfaction Measure to determine relevant issues. The Leisure Attitude Measurement may be helpful in identifying constraints due to attitude. Use Leisurescope Plus, Leisure Interest Measure, STILAP or other interest inventories to determine personal preferences.

Negative Terms to Aid Documentation

apathy	despairing	indifference	mechanical	miserable
blocked	emotional impoverishment	inhibited	melancholy	no interests
callous	emptiness	lack of satisfaction	minimal response	profoundly unhappy
cheerless	forlorn	low expectations	mirthless	troubled

Positive/Neutral Terms To Aid Documentation

enjoyment	gratification	in the state of flow	pleasurable	relish
fun	happy	intrinsic reward	preferable	stimulated

Flat Affect

Affective Domain

Problem	Goal	Objective	Intervention
Flat, depressed affect	To increase appropriate expressions of affect.	Patient will express self verbally 2 (4, 6) times each group.	Use expressive media as alternate means of expression. Engage in affect-enhancing activities: music, drama, reminiscence, areas which the patient has special skills, dance, social recreation and games.
		Patient will brighten on approach of therapists or friends 50% (75%, 100%) of the time.	Use humor.
		Patient will demonstrate affect appropriate to content of activity 50% (75%, 100%) of the time.	Encourage patient to talk about self: likes, dislikes, good times, etc.
		Patient will report on 1 (2, 3) events which have emotional content each day.	Use non judgmental, supportive approach.

Negative Terms to Aid Documentation

absence of spontaneity	humorless	labile	somber
apathetic	incongruous to situation	not spontaneous	unchanging
artificial	inconsistent	plastic	unrelated
bland	indifferent	shallow	unresponsive
bored	inhibited	smiles without warmth	unvarying
cheerless			
constrained			
diminished			
expressionless			
fixed affect			

Positive/Neutral Terms To Aid Documentation

congruent affect	normal range	range of emotions
face reflects emotions		relevant

Inappropriate Laughter
Affective Domain

Problem	Goal	Objective	Intervention
Inappropriate laughter	To use humor in appropriate ways.	Patient will demonstrate affect appropriate to content of activity 50% (75%, 100%) of the time. Patient will explain why s/he thought something was funny (and others didn't) when asked and discuss with therapist whether laughter really was appropriate on 50% (75%, 100%) of occasions.	Check to see if patient is hallucinating. Notify nursing staff or physician if necessary. Give patient feedback if laughter is inappropriate or incongruous to present activity. Confront superficial statements of patient. Ask what s/he really wants to say. This can cut through sarcasm or illicit a more thoughtful response.

Negative Terms to Aid Documentation

anti-social	hurtful	malicious	responding to internal
bizarre	illogical	manic	stimuli
demoralizing	intense	offensive	sexual preoccupation
detrimental	laughing binges	prejudicial	spontaneous
exaggerated	little or no insight	preservative behavior	traumatize
excessively boisterous	maleficent		unconstrained
			uncontrollable
			unhealthy
			unseen stimuli

Positive/Neutral Terms To Aid Documentation

amusing	droll	good sense of humor	not hurtful
comical	funny	healthy	relevant
congruent	genuine	mature	sincere
			sophisticated
			spontaneous

Treatment Plans

Overly Bright Affect
Affective Domain

Problem	Goal	Objective	Intervention
Overly bright affect	To have affect appropriate to content.	Patient will express self in a non-effusive manner in a group setting 50% (75%, 100%) of the time. Patient will share feelings and reasons for feelings in an appropriate manner 50% (75%, 100%) of the time when the feelings occur.	Tell patient that this emotional state doesn't seem appropriate to the situation. Tell patient that being overly bright is often a means of covering the pain inside. Give patient an opportunity to vent feelings. Use drama and other expressive modalities to practice the appropriate use of a variety of emotions. Use feelings chart/pictures to help patient identify current feeling.

Negative Terms to Aid Documentation

apparent	dramatic	expansive	grandiosity	unrealistic
artificial	effusive	expression deficit	laughing binges	
covering	elated	fantasy	out of touch with feelings	
cracks jokes	euphoric	frivolous	rapturous	

Positive/Neutral Terms To Aid Documentation

appropriate affect	cracks jokes	gregarious	non-effusive
cheerful	emphatic	in touch with feelings	relevant
congruent	expressing feelings well	justifiably sad	

Lability

Affective Domain

Problem	Goal	Objective	Intervention
Lability	To stabilize moods.	Patient will stabilize mood and resume activity with 1 (2, 3) cues from therapist 50% (75%, 100%) of the time. Patient will describe current emotion and be able to accurately state emotions during the previous 15 (30, 60) minutes to understand emotional states over a longer time span.	Listen to patient, use appropriate touch if a rapport has been established, then ask patient to identify ways of using this activity to increase positive feelings about self and to resume control. Refocus patient's attention to activity. Assist patients in learning healthy coping mechanisms. Work with patient to understand the difference between the mood of the moment and moods in a longer time frame.

Negative Terms to Aid Documentation

abrupt affect change	flight of emotions	pendulum	swaying	unstable
accelerated mood changes	intense	periods of	swing	vacillate
changeable	laughing binges	rapid fluctuation	switch	
excessive	oscillate	suppression	to and fro	

Positive/Neutral Terms To Aid Documentation

composure	easy-going	regulated	stable	temperate
control	even-tempered	restraint	steady	

Treatment Plans

Low Self Esteem

Affective Domain

Problem	Goal	Objective	Intervention
Low self-esteem	To increase self-esteem.	Patient will successfully complete 1 (2, 3) recreation projects or games each day.	Focus on success-oriented activities within the patient's ability range.
			Teach new skills as needed.
		Patient will make 1 (2, 3) positive statement(s) about self each group.	Furnish supplies and equipment.
		Patient will identify 3 (5, 10) personal strengths by (date).	Give patient positive feedback.
		Patient will learn one new skill (specify skill) by (date).	If patient does not initiate, ask for positive statement.
		Patient will provide 1 (2, 3) positive statements about self for each negative statement about self.	Ask patient to start a list of skills and abilities and to add to it each day.
			Examine patient's pattern of putting him/herself down.
			Help patient explore ways to feel good about self.

Negative Terms to Aid Documentation

criticism-sensitive	intimidated	personalizes	self-depreciating	self-pitying
evidence to contrary	misconception	presume	self-distrusting	sexual identify
identity	misperception	self-abnegation	self-effacing	vulnerable
impressionable	overwhelmed	self-blaming	self-image	

Positive/Neutral Terms To Aid Documentation

accepting	confidence	identity	secure	self-reliance
age appropriate	does not personalize	poise	self-approval	success producing tasks
autonomous	ego-enhancing	possesses ability	self-assurance	trust
avoids promotion of self	hopeful			

Cognitive Domain

1. Psychomotor Retardation
2. Ruminating Thought
3. Delusions or Hallucinations
4. Poor Concentration
5. Disorientation
6. Loose Associations
7. Poor Ego Boundaries
8. Poor Body Boundaries

Psychomotor Retardation
Cognitive Domain

Problem	Goal	Objective	Intervention
Psychomotor retardation, slow response to stimuli	To increase psychomotor activity.	Patient will respond to question within 10 (20, 30) seconds without additional cues 50% (75%, 100%) of the time.	Establish and maintain eye contact. State question or remark. Be patient, wait for response.
		Patient will participate in gross-motor activity 15 (30, 60) minutes each day.	Take patient's hand or touch arm to establish contact.
		Patient will increase reaction speed in activity (video game, shuttle runs, races, sewing, knitting, typing, jump rope) to perform 10% (20% 40%) more repetitions than his/her baseline score by (date).	Control environment, allowing appropriate level of distractions.
			Provide enjoyable activities where reaction speed is related to success.

Negative Terms to Aid Documentation

answer	dull	hesitancy	labor	slowed
apathetic	echo	hypoactive	lag behind	stall
awkward	falter	hypokinetic	lumbering	suspended animation
deceleration	gradual	indecision	slow on the uptake	tentative
delay	halting	irregular	slow-paced	unproductive

Positive/Neutral Terms To Aid Documentation

acceleration	energetic	make progress	reply
animated	enliven	quicken	tempo
answer	expeditious	reaction	vitality

Ruminating Thought

Cognitive Domain

Problem	Goal	Objective	Intervention
Ruminating thought	To decrease ruminating thoughts.	Patient will concentrate on activity 15 (30, 60) minutes without interruption due to ruminating thoughts.	Provide structured activities in groups and diversional activities to pursue in free time to engage attention.
		Patient will report interference of ruminating thoughts in daily activities has decreased to 50% (25%, 0%) of the time.	Reassure patient that s/he doesn't need to act on his/her impulses, that s/he has control of his/her behavior.
		Patient will initiate activities with other patients 1 (2, 3) times each day.	Encourage patient to initiate recreational activities in free time on unit with other patients.
			If not psychotic, teach relaxation and thought replacement techniques. Use cognitive therapy approach to reframe thinking.

Negative Terms to Aid Documentation

absorbed in the past	lacks follow through	perfectionist	preoccupation with detail	unrealistic, self-imposed
association of ideas	meditation	pondering	procrastinating	expectations
contemplation	over dependence on	poor decision making	repetitive themes	vacillating
free association	thought	premeditation	self-communing	
indecisive	pensive	preoccupation		

Positive/Neutral Terms To Aid Documentation

attentive to the present	concentrating	introspection	not preoccupied	relaxed
centered	focused on here and now	meditation	reasoning	released

Treatment Plans

Delusions or Hallucinations

Cognitive Domain

Problem	Goal	Objective	Intervention
Delusions, hallucinations	To increase reality functioning.	Patient will be able to state person, place, date and reason for being here 50% (75%, 100%) of the time.	Test patient's reality orientation by asking him/her to identify person, place, day, date and why group is assembled. Give reality orientation as needed.
		Patient will refocus attention to activity when instructed by therapist requiring 2 (4, 6) cues during a 60 minute activity.	Encourage reality testing from patient.
			Reassure patient that s/he is safe.
		Patient will respond in a congruent manner to activity 50% (75%, 100%) of the time during a 60 minute activity.	Do not negatively reinforce delusions with discussion.
			Refocus patient's attention back to structured activity.
			Draw patient into concrete, familiar activities to refocus attention.
			Avoid expressive media or focusing on feelings.
			Use structured activities with functional outcomes.

Negative Terms to Aid Documentation

absent	engrossed	flashback	jealousy	pressing
absorbed	exhibit	fragmented	magical thinking	substantial
alleged friend	extraordinary abilities	genuine	material	suspiciousness
assume as real	fabricate	grandiosity	misidentification	system of beliefs
concentration	fade	illusion	nonexistent	ungrounded
consuming	fantastic	imagined	optical illusion	urgency
daydreaming	fantasy	insubstantial	persecution	vision
disconnected	fascination	internal stimuli	phenomenon	without foundation
distorted body image	figment	invention	preoccupation	

Positive/Neutral Terms To Aid Documentation

actuality	engrossed	material	perceptible	useful
attentiveness	exhibit	objectivity	phenomenon	
concentration	factual	observable	practical	
concrete	genuine	palpable	tangible	

Poor Concentration
Cognitive Domain

Problem	Goal	Objective	Intervention
Poor concentration	To increase concentration.	Patient will attend to activity 5 (10, 20) minutes 1 (2, 3) times per day.	Establish patient's present attention span and help patient build up concentration by increasing increments of activity.
		Patient will increase number of items remembered from ____ (baseline) to ____ by ____ (date).	Use familiar or repetitive activities.
		Patient will continue to attend to an activity for 5 (10, 15) minutes in an environment with minimal (moderate) distractions.	If patient's attention wanders, encourage a 5 minute break then resume activity.
			Call patient by name to refocus attention.
			Use 1:1 activities in an environment which provides low stimulation.
			Use activities which require concentration for success.

Negative Terms to Aid Documentation

apathetic	distractible	immediate memory	needs cueing	resists redirection
attention not obtainable	doesn't absorb details	inattentiveness	neglecting	selective attention
brief intervals of attention	duration	lapses of attention	not engaged	stimulation overload
daydreams	extent	length of time	not observant	unable to ignore stimuli
detached	forgets instructions	low attending skill	oblivious	unaware
disorganized	ignores	misses	preoccupied	unheeding

Positive/Neutral Terms To Aid Documentation

age appropriate attention	concentrates on	heeds	observant	task persistence
application	duration	length of time	pays attention	vigilant
attentive	focus	listening	recalls	watches
capable of concentration	follows ___ step commands	noticing	redirectable	

Disorientation
Cognitive Domain

Problem	Goal	Objective	Intervention
Confusion, disorientation	To increase reality orientation.	Patient will correctly identify person, place, date 50% (75%, 100%) of the time.	Act as if condition is reversible.
			Check reality orientation, reorient as needed.
		Patient will follow simple 1 (2, 3) step instructions 50% (75%, 100%) of the time.	Provide information on date, time, location in a prominent location of the unit. Update it faithfully!
		Patient will recognize group leader and call him/her by name 50% (75%, 100%) of the time during activities.	Be patient, kind.
			Repeat instructions and redirect as needed.
		Patient will be able to find own (other) room 50% (75%, 100%) of the time.	Provide opportunities for finding locations in facility.
			Use validation techniques to develop rapport and calm.

Negative Terms to Aid Documentation

absent-minded	embarrassed	intensified confusion	poor comprehension	unable to distinguish
bewilderment	expresses doubts	long term memory	poor historian	unaware
cognitive decline	faulty recall	loss of pathfinding skills	puzzlement	unaware of current events
confusion	forgets details	loss of self care skills	quandary	unaware of surroundings
decreased concentration	forgets names	lost	rattled	uncertain
deficient memory	hesitant	misplaces familiar objects	recent past	unclear
detached	important events lost	non-sequential activities	requires prompting	unfamiliar
discountenance	inability to concentrate	pattern of memory deficits	sluggish recall	unimportant events lost
disorientation	inability to recall	perplexed	spotty memory	vague
distraction	inadequate	perseverates	time disorientation	
doesn't know season	indecisive	place, time, person	unable to cope	

Positive/Neutral Terms To Aid Documentation

acute	compensates	keen	recent memory
alert	familiar	long term memory	retention
aware	in contact	oriented	sharp
clear	in touch	place, time, person	structure

Treatment Plans

Loose Associations
Cognitive Domain

Problem	Goal	Objective	Intervention
Loose associations, tangential thinking	To increase thought organization.	Patient will respond with an answer relevant to discussion/conversation 50% (75%, 100%) of the time.	Tell patient you don't understand how what s/he is saying is connected to what was just discussed.
		Patient will complete 2 (3, 5) related steps in an activity by (date).	Provide structured step by step tasks.
		Patient will be able to provide 2 (3, 5) relevant associations to a topic of discussion 50% (75%, 100%) of the time.	Ask patient to rephrase what s/he wants to say.
			Avoid lengthy conversations about feelings.
			Focus on concrete ideas and functional activities. Avoid expressive media.

Negative Terms to Aid Documentation

affiliation	disorganized thought	jumbled thoughts	rambling
associational disorder	drifting	lack of logic	tangential
circular	incomprehensive	over-inclusive	unusual perspective
digressive	irrelevant	perseverative	word salad

Positive/Neutral Terms To Aid Documentation

able to restate	consistency	objective	refocus	structure
affiliation	germane	orderliness	relationship to topic	understands cause/effect
coherent	goal directed conversation	pertinent	relative	
conclude	linear thought patterns	rational	relevant	
connection	logical sequencing	redirected	sequential	

Poor Ego Boundaries

Cognitive Domain

Problem	Goal	Objective	Intervention
Poor ego boundaries	To increase ego boundaries.	Patient will remain calm when another patient is agitated 50% (75%, 100%) of the time.	Reassure patient that s/he is safe, that what is happening to another patient is not happening to him/her.
		Patient will be able to state the name of another patient who is having problems 50% (75%, 100%) of the time.	Provide calming, desensitizing activities.

Negative Terms to Aid Documentation

baffled	easily threatened	oneness	self	uncertain about role
bewildered	enmeshed	oversensitive	self-conscious	uncertain about situation
dependent	exhibit constraint	relationship	space	unsupportive
disconnect	inhibition	restriction	symbiotic	withdrawn
disjointed	insecure	rigidity of boundaries	sympathize	
easily aroused	limits	role confusion	thin-skinned	

Positive/Neutral Terms To Aid Documentation

apart from	detach	limits	secure	understand
clear-cut	disengaged	preserve	self	
confined	empathize	protected	self-concern	
congruent	empowerment	relationship	space	
curb	independent	restrained	stop	

Treatment Plans

Poor Body Boundaries
Cognitive Domain

Problem	Goal	Objective	Intervention
Poor body boundaries, i.e., bumping into other patients or staff, touching others	To increase patient's awareness of personal boundaries.	Patient will reduce touching of others to 5 (3, 1) instances a day (during an activity).	Use creative movement, dance, drama and exercise to facilitate increased awareness of self and body.
		Patient will not touch other patients.	Instruct patient in people's need for comfort zones.
		Patient will successfully get attention from another person without touching 1 (2, 3) times per day (activity).	Talk with patient about other people not wanting to be touched.
		Patient will be able to stand at a proper distance from others 50% (75%, 100%) of the time.	Emphasize appropriate distances between participants during activities.
			Describe other ways to get attention besides touching.

Negative Terms to Aid Documentation

area	comfort zone	impinges upon	touching	within reach
brush against	constraint	invading	unacceptable	
close	disengage	objectionable	uninvited	
close quarters	enmeshed	personal space	unpleasant	
collisions	impact	proximity	vicinity	

Positive/Neutral Terms To Aid Documentation

adequate	close	impact	proximity	vicinity
adjacent	comfort zone	invading	reduce	
area	conscious of …	limits	restrained	
awareness	constraint	personal space	touching	

Physical Domain

1. Psychomotor Retardation
2. Nonproductive Body Movements
3. Unsteady Gait
4. Unsteady Stance
5. Lethargy

Psychomotor Retardation
Physical Domain

Problem	Goal	Objective	Intervention
Psychomotor retardation, slow, rigid movements	To improve physical functioning.	Patient will engage in stretching exercise 10 (20, 30) minutes daily.	Stress full extension, stretching of muscles. Avoid fast, jerking movements.
		Patient will take a walk for 10 (20, 30) minutes with therapist three times a week.	Use music to increase interest and to slowly increase tempo of performance.
		Patient will catch and return a ball in simple game three times a week for a minimum of 10 (20, 30) minutes each time.	Use progressive gross-motor activity (i.e., exercise, tossing ball, dance or movement) with familiar music.
		Patient will participate in gross-motor activity 15 (30, 60) minutes each day.	Leader will increase speed gradually, asking patient to keep up pace.
		Patient will increase reaction speed in activity (video game, shuttle runs, races, sewing, knitting, typing, jump rope) to perform 10% (20%, 40%) more repetitions than his/her baseline score by (date).	Gradually increase complexity of activities.

Negative Terms to Aid Documentation

ambulation	dynamics	lag behind	mobility	slow-paced
anergenic	gradual	languid	plod	stiff
decelerate	hypoplasia	lessened ability	reach	strained
delayed	inertia	lethargic	restricted	struggling
difficulty with task	inhibited	listless	slow	tense
distort	laborious	locomotion	slow motion	uncoordinated
dulled expressiveness	lack of spontaneous action	lumbering	slow reactions	with effort

Positive/Neutral Terms To Aid Documentation

act	correction	heightened effort	preferable	self-restrained
advance	determination	improved	re-established	spontaneous
ambulation	develop	increased	recovery	synchronize
ameliorate	dynamics	locomotion	rectified	
attentive	energized	mobility	regulated	
composed	enhanced	moving	restored	

Nonproductive Body Movements
Physical Domain

Problem	Goal	Objective	Intervention
Anxious, nonproductive body movements	To decrease agitation.	Patient will stop anxious body movements with one prompting from staff 50% (75%, 100%) of the time.	Use gross-motor activities to relieve tension and other functional activities to engage attention.
		Patient will participate in appropriate gross motor activities 15 (30, 60) minutes a day.	Teach relaxation and breathing techniques when not contraindicated.
		Patient will participate in activity for 5 (10, 20) minutes without showing anxious behavior 50% (75%, 100%) of the time.	Provide patient with an alternative anxious behavior that is less distracting to the group if a multiple-step intervention is necessary (e.g., a seven inch long cloth ribbon to fidget with instead of tapping a pencil).
		Patient will participate in relaxation activities 3 (5, 7) times a week.	
		Patient will substitute less obtrusive movements for current anxious movements 50% (75%, 100%) of the time.	Encourage patients to talk about anxiety and useful stress reducers.

Negative Terms to Aid Documentation

acts out	excited	low frustration tolerance	self-grooming	unconscious movement
agitated	fidgets	moistens lips	self-hugging	uneasy
alarmed	fret	movement	startled	uninhibited movements
animated	generates	muscle tension	strain	unsettled
apprehensive	gestures	nail biting	sways	upset
can't sit still	high-strung	overwrought	tapping	vigorous
clears throat	impulsive	pacing	tendency	worried
clutching hands	inclination	perpetual movements	tense	wringing of hands
disquieted	jerky	prolific	troubled	writhing
distressed	jumpy	quicken	tumult	
disturbance	keeps moving	scratching	turmoil	

Positive/Neutral Terms To Aid Documentation

animated	calm	movement	relaxed	unworried
at ease	composed	not agitated	soothed	
at rest	modulated	productive movement	unconcerned	

Unsteady Gait
Physical Domain

Problem	Goal	Objective	Intervention
Unsteady gait, poor balance, shuffling gait.	To safely ambulate.	Patient will walk with assistance to/from activity without falling 100% of the time.	Walk with patient, allow patient to take leader's elbow or hand, if necessary.
		Patient will regain the ability to walk unassisted without falling by (date).	Restrict exercise to chair exercise or standing exercise with a chair for balance.
		Patient will practice (specific walking skill) taught by (other therapist) 1 (2, 3) times during activity each day.	Use range of motion and balance exercises.
			Observe patient closely. Avoid bending over exercises or moving head to left or right quickly.
			Refer patient to physical therapist for appropriate mobility aids.
			Provide activities which help patient practice compensatory skills taught by other therapists.

Negative Terms to Aid Documentation

abductor lurch	collides with objects	favors one leg	reels	treads
abnormality of gait	difficulty with inclines	fearful of falling	shaky	trips
antalgic gait	difficulty with uneven surfaces	footstep	shuffles	unstable
ataxic	dizzy	gait patterns	slap food gait	unsteady
awkward	equilibrium	heel strike	staggers	unsteady forward gait
broad-based stance	exaggerated stride	instability	stance	vertigo
careens	excessive	lurching	stumbles	walking pattern
center of gravity	falters	navigates	stumbling at intervals	wavers
characteristics		pigeon-toed	sways	weak side

Positive/Neutral Terms To Aid Documentation

center of gravity	equilibrium	gait patterns	stance	strides
characteristics	even	hip extension	steady	uniform steps
compensates	footstep	self-assured	step over	walking pattern

Unsteady Stance
Physical Domain

Problem	Goal	Objective	Intervention
Extremely unsteadiness, weakness, dizziness	To maintain patient safety.	Patient will not fall.	Refer to physical therapist for appropriate mobility aids.
		Patient will learn how to handle periods of dizziness or weakness so that s/he does not restrict activities more than necessary by (date).	Notify nursing service if fluctuation in balance occurs.
			Restrict activity level. Instruct patient to sit down.
			Use wheelchair to escort patient to and from activity until appropriate mobility aid is obtained.
			Monitor patient complaints and patient balance throughout activities. Look for trends related to medication times, time of day, etc.

Negative Terms to Aid Documentation

ambulation	falter	insecure	shaky	unsteadiness
antalgic gait	four-point gait	instability	staggers	vertigo
at risk	fragility	lightheadedness	sway	walking pattern
clumsiness	frail	mobility	three-point gait	width of gait
debilitation	hip extension	non-weight bearing	trips	
deterioration	impairment	profound	uncertainty of gait	
excessive	inclination to …	severe	unsafe	

Positive/Neutral Terms To Aid Documentation

ambulation	gait pattern	mobility	stabilize	utmost
endurance	hip extension	partial weight bearing	stance	walking pattern
firm	kinesthesia	positioning	strong	weight-bearing
full weight bearing	maximum	safe	transfer techniques	width of gait

Lethargy
Physical Domain

Problem	Goal	Objective	Intervention
Decreased activity level, lethargy	To increase energy.	Patient will engage in physical activity 1 (2, 3) times per day for 15 (30, 60) minutes.	Use exercise, walking, gross-motor games and sports.
		Patient will increase participation in 1 (2, 3) activities from passive to active by (date).	Encourage patient to engage in former leisure interests.
		Patient will add 1 (2, 3) activities to his/her schedule by (date).	Encourage patient to find new activities which are interesting.

Negative Terms to Aid Documentation

abstains	faltering	inertia	listless	static
apathetic	hesitant	lack of animation	minimize	takes it easy
avoiding	idle	languorous	passive	unengaged
curtailed	in the doldrums	lassitude	reduced	unoccupied
declining	inaction	lessened ability to …	reduced activity	vegetative
decreased	increments	lets things take their course	refrains	wavering
diminished	indecision	lets pass	sluggish	

Positive/Neutral Terms To Aid Documentation

active	attentive	engaged	increased activity level	participating
alert	augmentation	enhanced	increments	responds
amplification	develops	expanding	interacts	spontaneously
animated	energized	extension	maximizes	steps-up

Leisure Domain

1. Lack of Initiative
2. Few Leisure Interests
3. Poor Compliance with Personal Recreation Goals
4. Insufficient Participation
5. Multiple Stresses
6. Overwhelmed with Responsibilities
7. Few Social Supports
8. Knowledge Deficit
9. Requires Structure

Lack of Initiative

Leisure Domain

Problem	Goal	Objective	Intervention
Lack of initiative, dependence on others to plan activities	To increase initiative.	Patient will choose one activity to participate in during open recreation time and initiate that activity 1 (2, 3) times per day.	Help patient identify the recreational activities available on the unit.
			Have patient choose activity. Make suggestions if needed. Make sure choice has reasonable chance of success.
		Patient will set and meet daily goal for recreation participation 50% (75%, 100%) of the time.	Provide materials for independent use in unstructured time. Check on patient's progress daily.
		Patient will set and meet goal(s) for using a therapeutic leave of absence from the inpatient setting to pursue a recreational activity 1 (2, 3) times a week.	Structure therapeutic activities to engage patient.
			Suggest patient pair with another patient.
			Ask patient to identify a goal and list the steps necessary to accomplish the goal, i.e., getting physician approval, arranging transportation, possible companionship, etc.
			Discuss leave with patient upon return.

Negative Terms to Aid Documentation

apathetic	gives in	lacks progress	procrastinate	yields
dependent	inactive	passive	restricts	
deters	increment	postpone	submits	

Positive/Neutral Terms To Aid Documentation

accumulation	be active	establish	make progress	set out
add to	begin	expansion	maximize	sport
addition	boost	frolic	pastime	start
aim for	chose	hobbyist	plan ahead	take an active part in
ambition	commence	inclination	playfulness	targets
amuses	desire	increase	preferred	undertakes
aspires to …	enhances	increment	pursue	vitality
autonomy	enlarges	interdependent	push forward	volition

Few Leisure Interests

Leisure Domain

Problem	Goal	Objective	Intervention
Few identified leisure interests	To identify leisure interests.	Patient will complete leisure interest inventory by (date).	Use *Leisurescope Plus, STILAP, Leisure Interest Measure, Leisure Diagnostic Battery* or other standardized leisure interest testing tool.
		Patient will be able to list at least 3 (5, 7) activities that interest him/her by (date).	Use leisure education groups with peer support and suggestions to spark interests.
		Patient will identify 3, (5, 7) interests that s/he can pursue after discharge and begin to form a plan to be able to access them by (date).	Teach new leisure skills.
			Choose activities for groups with patient input and within patient's skill level.
			Provide 1:1 counseling.
			Assist patient in the development of skills necessary to locate community-based leisure opportunities.

Negative Terms to Aid Documentation

anhedonic	infrequency	lack of resources	rare
apathetic	insignificant	lack of skills	uncaring
dearth	lack of interest	limited selections	uncreative
eliminate	lack of motivation	poverty of activities	unusual

Positive/Neutral Terms To Aid Documentation

absorbing	discerning	free time	opportunity	resource knowledge
amusing	engrossing	game	pastime	spare time
appeals	entertaining	interest	perception	sport
appreciation	experience	knowledgeable	playfulness	understand
attention	familiar with	learning	recognition	unusual
comprehend	fascinating	leisure	recreation	well-rounded

Poor Compliance with Personal Recreation Goals

Leisure Domain

Problem	Goal	Objective	Intervention
Not meeting personal recreational goal	To increase follow-through.	Patient will accomplish personal goal 50% (75%, 100%) of the time. Patient will identify and overcome 1 (2, 3) barriers which prevented him/her from accomplishing a goal for recreation by (date).	Use reality therapy approach. Have the patient identify various steps to reaching the final goal. Use these as intermediate goals to allow practice setting and reaching goals. Remain non-judgmental. Ask patient when s/he expects to accomplish goal. Check on patient's progress at the agreed-upon time. Ask patient what prevented him/her from accomplishing the goal. Help patient problem-solve in order to achieve results.

Negative Terms to Aid Documentation

avoids	constraints	insincere	not committed	passive
barriers	fear	interest deficit	not well thought out	poor compliance
blocks	half finishes activity	isolative	obstruction	restraint
competitive player	hindrance	lack of knowledge about	opposition	restricted
complications	indifferent	lack of resources	over-stimulated	sporadic
compulsive	individual	limit	overwhelmed	unrealistic

Positive/Neutral Terms To Aid Documentation

accomplishes	coherence	follow through	playfulness	spectator
achievement	competitive player	from first to last	pleasurable activities	spontaneous
actuality	completion	fulfilled	practical	sport
aims for	comprehensive	genuine	produces	substantive
altogether	conclusion	hobby	purposeful	tangible change
ambition	culmination	individual	quality of play	target
amusement	engages in	involved with others	regularly participates	
attainment	entire	objectivity	satisfying leisure	
carries through	finish	pastime	sensible	

Insufficient Participation

Leisure Domain

Problem	Goal	Objective	Intervention
Insufficient participation in personal leisure interests, lack of interest	To increase interest and participation in gratifying leisure activities.	Patient will choose one leisure activity of interest and participate in it at least 30 minutes a day.	Review patient's leisure participation patterns. Use "Twenty Things I Like to Do", **Leisure Step Up** or similar leisure education and values clarification activities.
		Patient will resume personal interest (taking walks, carpentry, singing, needle craft, etc.) while in inpatient setting and participate at least 30 (60, 120) minutes each day.	Review benefits patient receives from preferred leisure activities.
		Patient will make 1 (3, 5) concrete plans for the use of free time after discharge.	Help patient identify present personal needs and identify how recreation can meet patient's needs (for relaxation, companionship, accomplishment, self-esteem, etc.).
			Help patient recognize lack of interest as symptom of mental illness. Offer choices, personal and material resources to patient.
			Have patient identify barriers to leisure participation, i.e., money, attitudes of significant others, transportation, lack of companionship, etc.
			Help patient problem solve to overcome barriers.
			Ask peers in leisure education group to assist with problem solving process.

Negative Terms to Aid Documentation

absence of	deficiency	inanimation	lack of incentive	no interest
abstains	hesitates	indecision	lacks initiative	poor follow through
apathy	inactivity	inertia	lassitude	unengaged
decline	inadequate	lack of	no gratification	wavering

Positive/Neutral Terms To Aid Documentation

amusement	free time	participate	recreation	sportive
committed	hobbyist	pastime	spare time	
engages in	initiative	playfulness	sport	

Behavioral Health Protocols

Multiple Stresses
Leisure Domain

Problem	Goal	Objective	Intervention
Multiple stresses at home or work	To compensate for stress.	Patient will demonstrate the ability to use a leisure activity to facilitate relaxation by reporting the perception of decreased stress after the activity 50% (75%, 100%) of the time.	Have patient identify present stresses and personal needs. Have patient identify recreational activities to use for stress management.
		Patient will list most significant stresses by (date).	Use enjoyable gross-motor and social activities.
		Patient will learn methods and coping mechanisms to deal with each significant stress by (date).	Teach relaxation techniques.

Teach time management techniques. |
| | | Patient will deal with stressful situations to his/her satisfaction 50% (75%, 100%) of the time. | |

Negative Terms to Aid Documentation

always planning	hurried	low level of exercise	restless	underestimates time
conflicts with ...	ignores reality	no time for self	rigid	unnecessary deadlines
detests wasting time	impatient	over schedules self	strain	unoccupied
disengaged	inability to relax	over-plans	stress tolerance	unproductive
estranged from supports	inflexible	over-working	struggle with ...	watches clock
fails to notice things	lives by deadlines	overuse of stimulants	talks rapidly	workaholic
guilt over relaxing	lives in the future	perfectionist	tension	
high impatience	low frustration tolerance	pressure	under pressure	

Positive/Neutral Terms To Aid Documentation

anger management	delayed gratification	focuses on quality of life	resources	takes time out
aptitude	easygoing	limits commitments	self-calming techniques	takes it easy
assertiveness	effective coping	modify	skills	takes time for relaxation
comfortable	escape coping	rational self-talk	slows down	tolerance for ambiguity
coping ability	experience	relaxes readily	social support system	tranquil

Overwhelmed with Responsibilities

Leisure Domain

Problem	Goal	Objective	Intervention
Overwhelmed with responsibilities, no leisure time	To increase leisure participation and satisfaction.	Patient will make a plan to take 30 minutes (1, 2 hours) for self each day by (date).	Ask patient to look at "workaholic" tendencies as a means of escaping and determine relevancy of this in his/her situation. When applicable, help patient identify patterns as symptomatic of adult children of alcoholics.
		Patient will make a realistic plan to have one night out each week by (date).	
		Patient will identify 1 (2, 3) barriers to participation in personal activities by (date).	Help patient role play or model assertive behavior, asking other family members to share responsibilities or improving employment situation.
		Patient will describe way to overcome 1 (2, 3) barriers by (date).	Help patient problem solve barriers, i.e., transportation, baby-sitters, money, etc.
		Patient will redefine "responsibilities" so they become opportunities for leisure instead of a burden (e.g., caring for an infant could be an opportunity to take a class on parenting with other supportive parents).	Help patient find support systems to share burdens and provide support for difficult times.

Negative Terms to Aid Documentation

avoids
commitments
deluged
distorted view of reality
encumbrance
evades
inaction
inundated
obligations
overburdened
overpowering
overtaxed
overwhelmed
overworked
responsibilities
stressed
terrified of no control

Positive/Neutral Terms To Aid Documentation

accountability
alleviates
be reconciled to
comfort in control
commitments
contentment
control is valued
cut back
cut down
dally
decline
decrease
diminish
ease
fulfillment
gratifies
lessen
mitigates
moderation
modify
not be serious
obligations
overcome
peace of mind
playfulness
pleased
reduction
relax
relieve
removal
respite
responsibilities
self-satisfaction
sense of responsibility
spare moments
spare time
tone down
yield

Few Social Supports
Leisure Domain

Problem	Goal	Objective	Intervention
Few social supports	To increase social supports.	Patient will initiate interaction with peers 1 (2, 3) times each group.	Structure group activities in dyads or small groups to give patient opportunity to practice social skills and increase self-confidence.
		Patient will identify 1 (2, 3) situations where or reasons why social support would make his/her life better by (date).	Role-play new situations to increase patient's comfort level.
		Patient will express healthy attitude about friendship by (date).	Discuss ways of feeling more comfortable in social settings.
		Patient will identify 3 ways to increase social supports and make friends after discharge by (date).	Use cognitive therapy techniques to help patient identify distortions about friendship and friendship interaction, then identify more rational responses.
			Ask patient to identify "safe" places to meet new people (i.e., support groups, leisure learning classes, clubs, church activities) where participants share common interests or values.

Negative Terms to Aid Documentation

avoidance
backward
bashful
church attendance only
clumsiness
co-dependent behavior
companionless
contrary to acceptable
  rules
control behaviors
dates compulsively
differentiate
distorted understanding
exclude

exploitive of others
false beliefs
fearful
immature
inadvertent
inappropriate
incapable
infrequent
insufficient
interested in dating but
intimidates
irresponsible behaviors
isolation
keeps aloof

keeps to self
little interest in others
lonely
lonesome
manipulates
meager
misleads others
nongregarious
occasional
promiscuous
puts on a face
reacts to hearsay
reclusive
reluctant

remote
resents limits
reserved
retiring
retreats
seclusion
self-centered
self-indulgent
shut off from …
shy
socially anxious
sole
solitude
sporadic

teases
thoughtless
threatens
unaffectionate
unapproachable
unmindful
unrealistic
unresponsive
unsociable
unthinking
withdraws

Positive/Neutral Terms To Aid Documentation

able to complement
able to listen
accepts feedback
acquaintances
amiable
anticipates
associates
association with …
be discerning
befriend
circle of acquaintances
circle of friends
classmates
clique

cohort
colleagues
common sense
companionable
companions
comprehends the expected
  behaviors
confidant
consensus reality
consequences
cultivates friendship
dealings with
deliberate

discrimination of
  right/wrong
exchange
familiarity
family support
friendliness
friends
give-and-take
greeting
harmony
has basic social
  conventions
hospitality
identifies self as likable

interactional processes
interpersonal behaviors
intimate
learns from experience
long-term relationships
make friends with …
plans ahead
playmates
progressive relationships
realistic social judgment
receives complements
reconcile
refrains from gossip
roommates

schoolmates
sensitive
sociable
social circle
social performance
socially acceptable
  behaviors
street-smart
supportive of others
thinks ahead
thoughtful
trusted by others

Knowledge Deficit
Leisure Domain

Problem	Goal	Objective	Intervention
Insufficient information about community resources	To increase awareness of community resources.	Patient will learn about 1 (3, 5) community resources to fit his/her needs by (date). Patient will make 1 (3, 5) telephone calls to gather information and initiate involvement with community resources by (date).	Review community resources that patient can follow-up on. Ask patient to do the investigating while in inpatient setting. Offer use of telephone. Assist patient with skills required to use phones, voice mail and other technologies as needed.

Negative Terms to Aid Documentation

clueless	deficiency	inadequate
dearth	ignorant	insufficient
		lack of
		not enough

Positive/Neutral Terms To Aid Documentation

acquire	describe	need	requirements
call	detail	notification	scholarships available
clubs	familiarize	orientation	self-learner
coach in	free entertainment	outline	society
communication	initiate	parks department	sports center
community	knowledge	prepare	support groups
community center	learn	recount	telephone
confidence	low cost recreation	rehearse	telephone numbers
			transportation system
			voice mail
			where to shop
			White Pages
			write
			Yellow Pages

Requires Structure
Leisure Domain

Problem	Goal	Objective	Intervention
Needs structured, day activities after discharge (Patient takes insufficient initiative in using free time constructively.)	To increase daily structure.	Patient will structure current day and follow through with plans 50% (75%, 100%) of the time. Patient will have plans for structure of days, weeks and months to use after discharge by (date).	Identify amount of structure required and the range of fluctuation in the patient's functional ability to help formulate a good placement Recognize that schedules have daily, weekly, monthly and yearly components. Work with patient and social service worker to set up activities such as day treatment or adult day health care.

Negative Terms to Aid Documentation

confused	immobilized by fear	instability of emotions	may become victim	thought disorder
decreased ability	impaired judgment	intense and sudden actions	memory impairment	unexplainable changes
delusions	impulsive purchases	judgment impairment	no insight	unpredictable
disoriented	inability in basic ADLs	labile	orientation problems	vacillating reactions
does not feed self	inappropriate use of 911	lack of compensation	poor pathfinding skills	wanders
erratic	incapacitated	lacks competence	relies heavily on others	
fluctuating orientation	incompetent	loss of reading ability	superficial relationships	

Positive/Neutral Terms To Aid Documentation

advanced ADLs	control of emotions	organization	regular	understands situation
arrangement	direction	pattern	simple math	
attendant	disposition	perception of situations	structure	
carry out	effective decisions	reality contact	supervision	
consistency	follow through	recognition of money	systematic	

Treatment Plans

147

References

American Psychiatric Association. 1994. **Diagnostic and Statistical Manual of Mental Disorders (Fourth Edition)**. Washington, DC.

Antonucci, T. C. 1989. "Social Support Influences on the Disease Process." In L. Carstensen and J. Neale (Eds.) **Mechanisms of Psychological Influence on Physical Health**. (pp. 23-41). New York: Plenum Press.

Armstrong, M. and S. Lauzen. 1994. **Community Integration Program**. Ravensdale, WA: Idyll Arbor, Inc.

Ascher-Svanum, H. and A. A. Krause. 1991. **Psychoeducational Groups for Patients with Schizophrenia: A Guide for Practitioners**. Rockville: Aspen Publications.

Baldwin, B. 1985. **It's All In Your Head: Lifestyle Management Strategies for Busy People**. Wilmington, NC: Direction Dynamics.

Banzinger, G. and S. Rousch. 1983 "Nursing homes for the birds: A control-relevant intervention with bird feeders." *The Gerontologist*, 23, 527-531.

Benson, H. 1975. **Relaxation Response**. New York: Avon Books.

Benson, H. and E. Stuart. 1992. **The Wellness Book: A Comprehensive Guide to Maintaining Health and Treating Stress-Related Illness**. New York: Birch Lane Press.

Benson, H., I. Kutz and J. Borysenko. 1985. "Meditation and Psychotherapy: a Rationale for the Integration of Dynamic Psychotherapy, the Relaxation Response and Mindfulness Meditation." *American Journal of Psychiatry*. 142 (1) 1-8.

Best-Martini, E., M. A. Weeks and P. Wirth. 1994. **Long Term Care: Interpretation and Inspiration for Activity and Social Service Professionals**. Ravensdale, WA: Idyll Arbor, Inc.

Birren, J. E. and Deutchman, D. E. 1991. **Guiding Autobiography Groups for Older Adults**. Baltimore: Johns Hopkins Press.

Blauvelt, C. T. and F. Nelson. 1990. **A Manual of Orthopaedic Terminology, Fourth Edition**. St. Louis: C. V. Mosby Company.

Bullock, C. C. and C. Z. Howe. 1991. "A model therapeutic recreation program for the reintegration of persons with disabilities in the community." *Therapeutic Recreation Journal*. 25,(1) 7-17.

burlingame, j. and T. M. Blaschko. 1990. **Assessment Tools for Recreational Therapy**. Ravensdale, WA: Idyll Arbor, Inc.

Burns, D. D. 1989. **The Feeling Good Handbook**. New York: Wm. Morrow & Company, Inc.

Carrigan, P., G. H. Collinger, Jr., H. Benson, H. Robinson, L. W. Wood, P. M. Lehrer, R. L. Woolfolf and J. W. Cole. 1980. "The use of meditation — relaxation techniques for the management of stress in a working population." *Journal of Occupational Medicine*. 22 (4), 221-231.

Compton, D. M. and S. E. Iso-Ahola (Eds.) 1994. **Leisure and Mental Health**. Park City, UT: Family Development Resources, Inc.

Coyle, C. P., W. B. Kinney, B. Riley and J. W. Shank. 1991. **Benefits of Therapeutic Recreation: A Consensus View**. Ravensdale, WA: Idyll Arbor, Inc.

Daems J. (Ed.) 1994. **Reviews of Research in Sensory Integration**. Torrance: Sensory Integration International.

Davis, M., E. Robbins Eshelman and M. McKay. 1995. **The Relaxation and Stress Reduction Workbook, Fourth Edition**. Oakland, CA: New Harbinger Publications.

Dehn, D. 1995. **Leisure Step Up**. Ravensdale, WA: Idyll Arbor, Inc.

de Vries, H. A. 1987. Tension Reduction with Exercise. In Wm. P. Morgan and S. E. Goldston (Eds.). **Exercise and Mental Health**. Washington, DC: Hemisphere Publishing

Eisler, R. M., M. Hersen, and P. M. Miller. 1974. "Shaping components of Assertive Behavior with Instruction and Feedback." *American Journal of Psychiatry*. 131, 1344-1347.

Epperson, A., P. A. Witt and G. Hitzhusen. 1977. **Leisure Counseling: An Aspect of Leisure Education**. Springfield: Charles C. Thomas.

Feil, N. 1993. **The Validation Breakthrough: Simple Techniques for Communicating with People with Alzheimer's-Type Dementia**. Baltimore: Health Professions Press.

Ferguson, D. D. 1991. "The development of therapeutic recreation protocols through a systematic process." Unpublished paper presented at the Midwest Symposium for Therapeutic Recreation. Oconomowoc. WI.

Ferguson, D. D. 1994. "Developing protocols for leisure problems in mental health." In D. A. Compton and S. E. Iso-Ahola (Eds.). **Leisure and Mental Health** (pp. 277-292). Park City, UT: Family Development Resources, Inc.

Gabor, D. 1983. **How to Start a Conversation and Make Friends**. New York: Simon and Schuster.

Gallo, J. J., W. Reichel and L. Andersen. 1988. **Handbook of Geriatric Assessment**. Rockville, MD: Aspen Publications.

Greist, J. H., M. H. Klein, R. R. Eischens, A. S. Gurman and W. P. Morgan. 1979. "Running as a treatment for depression." *Comprehensive Psychiatry*, 20, 41-54.

Grossman, A. H. 1976. "Power of Activity in a Treatment Setting." *Therapeutic Recreation Journal*. 10 (4), 119-124.

Hipp, E. 1985. **Fighting Invisible Tigers: A Stress Management Guide for Teens**. Minneapolis: Free Spirit Publishing.

Hipp, E. 1987. **A Teacher's Guide to Fighting Invisible Tigers: A 12 Part Course in Lifeskills Development**. Minneapolis: Free Spirit Publishing.

Hurley, O. 1988. **Safe Therapeutic Exercise for the Frail Elderly: An Introduction**. Albany: The Center for the Study of Aging.

Kane, R. and R. Kane. 1981. **Assessing the Elderly, A Practical Guide to Measurement**. Lexington: Lexington Books.

Karam, C. 1989. **A Practical Guide to Cardiac Rehabilitation**. Rockville, MD: Aspen Publishers, Inc.

Kaufman, G. and L. Raphael. 1990. **Stick Up for Yourself! Every Kid's Guide to Personal Power and Positive Self-Esteem**. Minneapolis: Free Spirit Publishing.

Kaufman, G. and L. Raphael. 1991. **Teacher's Guide to Stick Up for Yourself! A 10 Part Course In Self-Esteem and Assertiveness for Kids**. Minneapolis: Free Spirit Publishing.

Kemp, B. 1990. **Geriatric Rehabilitation**. Boston: College-Hill Press.

Keogh-Hoss, M. A. 1994. **Therapeutic Recreation Activity Assessment**. Ravensdale, WA: Idyll Arbor, Inc.

Kloseck, M. and Lammers. 1989. "Leisure Competence Measure." (A cooperative research project between Parkwood Hospital, London, Ontario, Canada and Oklahoma State University, Oklahoma.)

Knight, L. and D. Johnson. 1991. "Therapeutic recreation protocols; patient problem centered approach." In R. Riley (Ed.). **Quality Management: Applications for Therapeutic Recreation** (pp. 17-150). State College, PA: Venture Publishing, Inc.

Korb, K. L., S. D. Azok and E. A. Leutenberg. 1992. **SEALS + Plus: Self-Esteem and Life Skills: Reproducible Activity-Based Handouts Created for Teachers and Counselors**. Beachwood, OH: Wellness Reproductions, Inc.

Leavy, R. L. 1983. "Social Support and Psychological Disorder." *Journal of Community Psychology*, 11, 3-21.

Liberman, R. P., F. J. Lillie, I. R. H. Falloon, E. J. Harpin, W. Hutchison and B. A. Stout. 1984. "Social skills training for relapsing schizophrenics. An experimental analysis." *Behavioral Modification*. 8, 155-179.

Martinsen, E. W., A. Medhus and L. Sandvik. 1984. "The effect of aerobic exercise on depression: A controlled study." Unpublished manuscript.

Matheny, K. S., D. W. Aycock, J. Pugh, W. L. Curlette and K. A. Silva Cannella. 1986. "Stress Coping: A Qualitative and Quantitative Synthesis and Implications for Treatment." *The Counseling Psychologist*. 14 (4) 499-549.

McGlynn, G. 1987. **Dynamics of Fitness: A Practical Approach**. Dubuque, IA: Wm. C. Brown.

Morgan, W. P. and S. E. Goldston. 1987. **Exercise and Mental Health**. Washington, DC: Hemisphere Publishing.

Olsson, R. H., Jr. 1990. **Recreational Therapy Protocol Design: A Systems Approach to Treatment Evaluation**. Toledo, OH: International Leisure Press.

Parker, S. D. and C. Will. 1993. **Activities for the Elderly Volume 2: A Guide to Working with Residents with Significant Physical and Cognitive Disabilities**. Ravensdale, WA: Idyll Arbor, Inc.

Russoniello, C. V. 1991. "An exploratory study of physiological and psychological changes in alcoholic patients after recreation therapy treatments." Paper presented at the Benefits of Therapeutic Recreation in Rehabilitation Conference, Lafayette Hill, PA.

Scogin, F. and M. Prohaska. 1993. **Aiding Older Adults with Memory Complaints**. Sarasota: Professional Resource Press.

Searle, M. S. and M. J. Mahon. 1991. "Leisure education in a day hospital: The effects on selected social-psychological variables among older adults." *Canadian Journal of Community Mental Health*. 10(2), 95-109.

Searle, M. S. and M. J. Mahon. 1993. "The effects of a leisure education program on selected social-psychological variables: A three month follow-up investigation." *Therapeutic Recreation Journal*, 27 (1), 9-21.

Shary, J. and S. Iso-Ahola. 1989. "Effects of a control relevant intervention program on nursing home residents' perceived competence and self-esteem." *Therapeutic Recreation Journal*. 23, 7-16.

Sime, W. E. 1987. "Exercise in the treatment and prevention of depression." In W. P. Morgan and S. E. Goddamn (Eds.) **Exercise and Mental Health** (pp. 145-152). Washington DC: Hemisphere Publishing.

Skalko, T. K. 1982. "The effects of leisure education program on the perceived leisure well-being of psychiatrically impaired active army personnel." Unpublished doctoral dissertation. University of Maryland: College Park, MD.

Smith-Marker, C. G. 1988. **Setting Standards for Professional Nursing: the Marker Model**. Baltimore: Resource Applications.

Taylor, C. B., J. F. Sallis and R. Needle. 1985. "The relation of physical activity and exercise to mental health." *Public Health Reports*. 100, 195-202.

Turner, R. J. 1981. "Social Support as a Contingency in Psychological Well-Being." *Journal of Health and Social Behavior*. 22, 357-367.

Wassman, K. B. and S. E. Iso-Ahola. 1985. "The relationship between recreation participation and depression in psychiatric patients." *Therapeutic Recreation Journal.* 19 (3), 63-70.

Winnick, J. P. (Ed.) 1990. **Adapted Physical Education and Sport**. Champaign: Human Kinetics Books.

Wittals, H. and J. Greisman. 1971. **The Clear and Simple Thesaurus Dictionary**. New York: Grosset and Dunlap, Publishers.

Wong, S. E., M. D. Terranova, L. Bowen and R Zarate. 1987. "Providing independent recreational activities to reduce stereotypic vocalization in chronic schizophrenics." *Journal of Applied Behavior Analysis.* 20, 77-81.

Wong, S. E., M. D. Terranova, B. D. Marshall, L. K. Banzett and R. P. Liberman. 1983. "Reducing bizarre stereotypic behavior in chronic psychiatric patients: Effects of supervised and independent recreational activities." Presented at the Ninth Annual Convention of the Association of Behavior Analysis, Milwaukee, WI.

Young, J. T. 1986. "A Cognitive-Behavioral Approach to Friendship Disorders." In V. J. Derlego and B. A. Winstead. **Friendship in Social Interaction**. (pp. 247-276). New York: Springer-Verlag.

Zgola, J. M. 1987. **Doing Things: A Guide to Programming Activities for Persons with Alzheimer's Disease and Related Disorders**. Baltimore: Johns Hopkins Press.

Zimbardo, P. 1977. **Shyness: What It Is. What to Do About It**. Reading, MA: Wesley Publishing Company.